CATIA® V6
ESSENTIALS

KOGENT LEARNING SOLUTIONS, INC.

JONES AND BARTLETT PUBLISHERS

Sudbury, Massachusetts

BOSTON   TORONTO   LONDON   SINGAPORE

World Headquarters

Jones and Bartlett Publishers
40 Tall Pine Drive
Sudbury, MA 01776
978-443-5000
info@jbpub.com
www.jbpub.com

Jones and Bartlett Publishers
Canada
6339 Ormindale Way
Mississauga, Ontario L5V 1J2
Canada

Jones and Bartlett Publishers
International
Barb House, Barb Mews
London W6 7PA
United Kingdom

Jones and Bartlett's books and products are available through most bookstores and online booksellers. To contact Jones and Bartlett Publishers directly, call 800-832-0034, fax 978-443-8000, or visit our website www.jbpub.com.

Substantial discounts on bulk quantities of Jones and Bartlett's publications are available to corporations, professional associations, and other qualified organizations. For details and specific discount information, contact the special sales department at Jones and Bartlett via the above contact information or send an email to specialsales@jbpub.com.

Production Credits

Publisher: David Pallai
Editorial Assistant: Molly Whitman
Production Assistant: Ashlee Hazeltine
Associate Marketing Manager: Lindsay Ruggiero
V.P., Manufacturing and Inventory Control:
   Therese Connell
Composition: diacriTech

Art Rendering: diacriTech
Cover and Title Page Design: Scott Moden
Cover Image: © Malinovskyy Kostyantyn/
   ShutterStock, Inc.
Printing and Binding: Malloy, Inc.
Cover Printing: Malloy, Inc.

Library of Congress Cataloging-in-Publication Data
CATIA V6 essentials/Kogent Learning Solutions, Inc.
   p. cm.
   Includes index.
   ISBN-13: 978-0-7637-8516-1 (pbk.)
   ISBN-10: 0-7637-8516-4 (ibid.)
   1. Computer-aided engineering–Computer programs. 2. CATIA (Computer file) I. Kogent Learning Solutions, Inc.
   TA345.C3863 2009
   620'.00420285536–dc22
                                    2009035568

6048
Printed in the United States of America
13 12 11 10 09   10 9 8 7 6 5 4 3 2 1

TABLE OF CONTENTS

1

GETTING STARTED WITH CATIA V6

In This Chapter

◊ Key Enhancements in CATIA V6
◊ Installing CATIA V6
◊ Opening CATIA V6
◊ Starting a Workbench in CATIA V6
◊ Exploring the CATIA V6 User Interface
◊ Summary

Computer Graphics-Aided Three-Dimensional Interactive Application (CATIA) is the world's leading computer-aided design (CAD)/computer-aided manufacturing (CAM)/computer-aided engineering (CAE) package. Developed by Dassault Systèmes and marketed worldwide by IBM, CATIA delivers one of the best Product Lifecycle Management (PLM) solutions. It provides a single platform to design, analyze, and manufacture a product; this makes the product development faster and easier. CATIA is used by various industries, including automobiles, aerospace, industrial equipment, and ship building.

CATIA Version 6 (V6) was first released in mid-2008. The latest release of CATIA V6 is CATIA V6R2009, which was launched on November 25, 2008. The new CATIA V6 user interface allows designers to directly work with solid models rather than using the feature-based design approach of CATIA V5.

In this chapter, you first learn about the key enhancements introduced in CATIA V6. Then, you learn how to install CATIA V6 on your computer. Further, you learn how to open CATIA V6 and how to start a new workbench in CATIA V6. Finally, various components of the user interface of CATIA V6 are discussed in detail.

We begin with the key enhancements in CATIA V6.

1.1 KEY ENHANCEMENTS IN CATIA V6

A number of enhancements were made to CATIA V6 to make the process of product development easier and faster as compared to the previous versions of CATIA. The key enhancements made in CATIA V6 are as follows:

- Global collaborative innovation
- Real-time working environment
- Single platform for product development
- Systems engineering improvements

We discuss each of these enhancements in detail.

Global Collaborative Innovation

The users of CATIA V6 can access the collaborative three-dimensional (3D) environment of Dassault Systèmes that allows an unlimited number of online users from all over the world to participate in the virtual 3D brainstorming conference. Once connected, users can use the online collaborative tools available for 3D brainstorming to co-review and co-design the product. With CATIA V6, designers, engineers, and even the prospective users of the product are able to collaborate on the product in such a way as if they were together in the same room. CATIA also supports asynchronous collaboration among users, which means that even the offline users can share the changes made in the product.

Real-Time Working Environment

CATIA V6 provides a unique real-time working environment to design highly realistic 3D models. For example, it allows different groups of users, related to customer services, technical training, and maintenance operations, to interact with each other and create enhanced 3D-based composite documents for all types of products by using their company's existing PLM investments. It also provides new materials, effects, and paint shaders to give a realistic appearance to virtual models.

Single Platform for Product Development

A new product goes through various stages from design to manufacturing during its development life cycle. CATIA V6 reduces the complexity of developing a product by allowing the integration of various product development approaches within a single platform. It allows you to store the data related to all the phases, such as designing and manufacturing, of a project at a single place from where it can be accessed and used by the designers, engineers, and manufacturers working on the project.

Systems Engineering Improvements

Systems engineering has evolved as a collective, integrated, and multidisciplinary model for product development to manage the increasing complexity of products and projects. It enables you to produce systems that satisfy customer needs and reduce risk as well as the costs associated with the development of a project. CATIA V6 has introduced a unique requirements, functional, logical, and physical (RFLP) approach that provides a comprehensive and collaborative definition across different views (requirements, functional, logical, and physical) of a product. In other words, the RFLP approach simplifies the product development process by allowing you to work on different views of a product by bringing them together on the same platform.

After becoming familiar with the key enhancements in CATIA V6, we learn how to install CATIA V6.

1.2 INSTALLING CATIA V6

Before beginning the installation process, ensure that your computer meets the minimum hardware and software requirements for installing CATIA V6. You also need Microsoft .NET Framework 3.0 (or higher) and Java v5 (or higher) installed on your computer.

Table 1.1 shows the minimum hardware and software requirements for installing CATIA V6:

Component	Requirements
Processor	Intel Pentium 4 (optional Dual Core), Intel Xeon (optional Dual Core), Intel Core 2 Duo, Intel Quad Core-based workstations running 32-bit Windows versions, Intel Pentium 4 EM64T (optional Dual Core), Intel Xeon EM64T (optional Dual Core), Intel Core 2 Duo, Intel Quad Core EM64T, Intel Quad Core Xeon EM64T, AMD Opteron (Series 100 minimum, optional Dual Core)-based workstations running 64-bit Windows versions.
Memory	512 MB of RAM for Windows XP Professional Edition SP2 2 GB of RAM for Windows Vista Business Edition and Windows Vista Enterprise Edition. 4 GB of RAM for Windows XP Professional x64 Edition SP2, Windows Vista Business 64-bit Edition, and Windows Vista Enterprise 64-bit Edition.
Hard Disk	The minimum recommended hard disk space of 4 GB is required to store program executables, program data, and usage environment.

TABLE 1.1   System requirements for installing CATIA V6

Continued

Component	Requirements
Removable Storage	A CD or DVD drive for installation from disk.
Network Adapter	An active Ethernet adapter is required for licensing purposes.
Display	A graphic color display that is compatible with the selected platform-specific graphic adapter. The minimum resolution for Windows workstations is 1280×1024.
Graphic Adapter	A graphic adapter with a 3D OpenGL accelerator is required.
Pointing Device	A three-button mouse is required as a pointing device.
Operating System	Windows XP, Windows Vista.

TABLE 1.1   System requirements for installing CATIA V6

Now, perform the following steps to install CATIA V6:

1. *Insert* the CATIA V6 DVD into your DVD-ROM and *double-click* the **setup. exe** file. A message box opens, as shown in **Figure 1.1**:

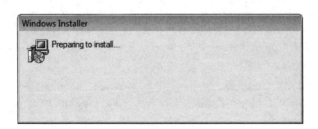

FIGURE 1.1

After a few minutes, the **CATIA V6R2009 Welcome** window opens (**Figure 1.2**).

2. *Click* the **Next** button to continue, as shown in Figure 1.2:

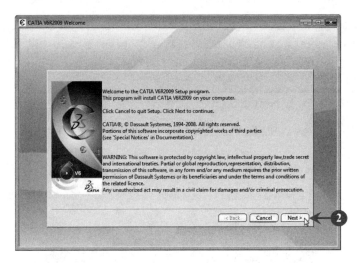

FIGURE 1.2

The **CATIA V6R2009 License** window opens (**Figure 1.3**).

3. *Click* the **Next** button to continue, as shown in Figure 1.3:

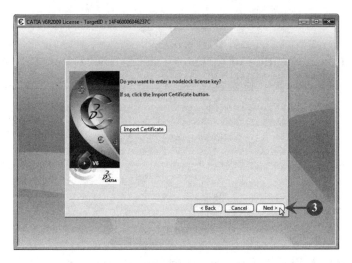

FIGURE 1.3

The **CATIA V6R2009 Choose Destination Location** window opens, displaying the location of the destination folder to install CATIA V6 (**Figure 1.4**).

> **Note:** You can select another folder on your computer to install CATIA V6 by *clicking* the **Browse** button. In any case, the destination folder should be empty.

4. *Click* the **Next** button to continue, as shown in Figure 1.4:

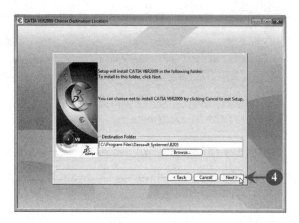

FIGURE 1.4

The **Confirm creation of directory** message box opens (**Figure 1.5**).

5. *Click* the **Yes** button to close the **Confirm creation of directory** message box, as shown in Figure 1.5:

FIGURE 1.5

The **CATIA V6R2009 Choose Environment Location** window opens, displaying the location of the environment directory for CATIA V6 (**Figure 1.6**).

> **Note:** You can select another folder on your computer as the environment directory for CATIA V6 by *clicking* the **Browse** button.

6. *Click* the **Next** button to continue, as shown in Figure 1.6:

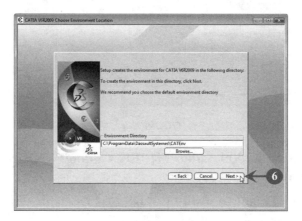

FIGURE 1.6

The **Confirm creation of directory** message box opens (**Figure 1.7**).

7. *Click* the **Yes** button to close the **Confirm creation of directory** message box, as shown in Figure 1.7:

FIGURE 1.7

The **CATIA V6R2009 Setup Type** window opens, providing you options to choose a setup type (**Figure 1.8**).

8. *Select* a setup type: **Complete** or **Custom** (Figure 1.8). In our case, we have kept the default option, **Complete**, selected.

9. *Click* the **Next** button to continue, as shown in Figure 1.8:

FIGURE 1.8

The **CATIA V6R2009 Video MJPEG Codec/Filter installation** window opens (**Figure 1.9**).

10. *Select* the **I want to install the DS MJPEG codec/filter package** check box (Figure 1.9).

11. *Click* the **Next** button to continue, as shown in Figure 1.9:

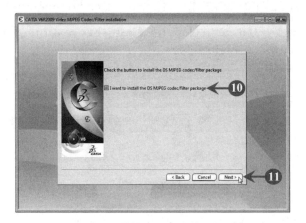

FIGURE 1.9

The **CATIA V6R2009 Choose Communication Ports** window opens (**Figure 1.10**).

12. *Click* the **Next** button to continue, as shown in Figure 1.10:

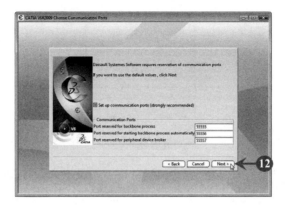

FIGURE 1.10

The **CATIA V6R2009 Data directories selection** window opens, asking you to enter the Java home path (**Figure 1.11**).

13. *Click* the **Browse** button to select the Java home path on your computer, as shown in Figure 1.11:

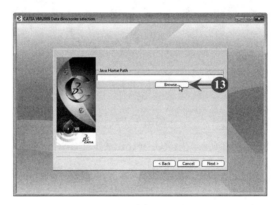

FIGURE 1.11

The **Select Directory** dialog box opens (**Figure 1.12**).

14. *Browse* and *select* a Java Runtime Environment (JRE) folder present on your computer (Figure 1.12). In our case, we have selected the **jre1.6.0_05** folder.

15. *Click* the **OK** button to close the **Select Directory** dialog box, as shown in Figure 1.12:

FIGURE 1.12

The Java Home Path on your computer gets added to the Java Home Path text box in the **CATIA V6R2009 Data directories selection** window (**Figure 1.13**).

16. *Click* the **Next** button to continue, as shown in Figure 1.13:

FIGURE 1.13

The **CATIA V6R2009 Custom Shortcut Creation** window opens (**Figure 1.14**).

17. *Click* the **Next** button to continue, as shown in Figure 1.14:

FIGURE 1.14

The **CATIA V6R2009 Start Copying Files** window opens (**Figure 1.15**).

18. *Click* the **Install** button to continue, as shown in Figure 1.15:

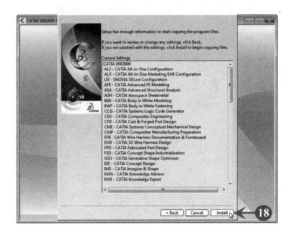

FIGURE 1.15

The **CATIA V6R2009 Setup** window opens, displaying the progress of the CATIA V6 installation process, as shown in **Figure 1.16**:

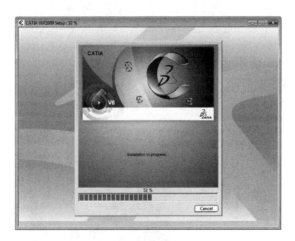

FIGURE 1.16

After the CATIA V6 installation process is finished, the **CATIA V6R2009 Setup Complete** window opens displaying a message indicating that CATIA V6R2009 has been installed on your computer (**Figure 1.17**). You can also notice in Figure 1.17 that the **I want to launch CATIA V6R2009 now** check box is selected by default. This will launch CATIA V6 after the **CATIA V6R2009 Setup Complete** window is closed. If you do not want to start CATIA V6 now, clear the **I want to launch CATIA V6R2009 now** check box.

19. *Click* the **Finish** button to close the **CATIA V6R2009 Setup Complete** window, as shown in Figure 1.17:

FIGURE 1.17

After learning to install CATIA V6, we now learn to open it.

1.3 OPENING CATIA V6

Once you have installed CATIA V6 on your computer, you can open it to see how to work with it. In CATIA V6, each CATIA file that you work with is stored as an object, rather than as a document, in a database. This ensures improved working of the PLM cycle and also allows multiple users to simultaneously work on a single product.

Perform the following steps to open CATIA V6:

1. *Select* **Start > All Programs > CATIA > CATIA V6R2009**, as shown in **Figure 1.18**:

FIGURE 1.18

The user interface of CATIA V6 opens along with the **Connect** dialog box (**Figure 1.19**). This dialog box allows you to select a data source to store your design data, a user name, and a password. If you select a 3D XML data source, you need not enter a user name and password.

2. *Click* the **More** button in the **Connect** dialog box to select a data source, as shown in Figure 1.19:

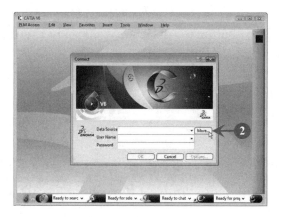

FIGURE 1.19

The **Discovery** dialog box opens (**Figure 1.20**).

3. *Click* the **Add New Connection** button to add a new connection, as shown in Figure 1.20:

FIGURE 1.20

The **Add Connection(1/2)** dialog box opens (**Figure 1.21**).

4. *Select* a connection type from the **Connection Type** drop-down list. In our case, we have selected **3D XML** as the connection type, as shown in Figure 1.21:

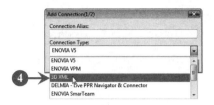

FIGURE 1.21

5.   *Click* the **Next** button to continue, as shown in **Figure 1.22**:

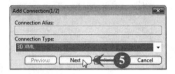

FIGURE 1.22

The **Add Connection(2/2)** dialog box opens (**Figure 1.23**).

6.   *Click* the **Find** button to select the path of the 3D XML file, as shown in Figure 1.23:

FIGURE 1.23

The **FileSelector** dialog box opens (**Figure 1.24**).

7.   *Browse* and *select* the 3D XML file, **Sample**, from the **C:\Program Files\ Dassault Systemes\B205\intel_a\resources\3DXMLModels** folder using the **Look in** combo box (Figure 1.24).

8.   *Click* the **Open** button, as shown in Figure 1.24:

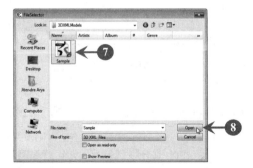

FIGURE 1.24

The **FileSelector** dialog box closes and the path of the **Sample.3dxml** file gets added to the **Add Connection(2/2)** dialog box (**Figure 1.25**).

9. *Click* the **Finish** button to close the **Add Connection(2/2)** dialog box, as shown in Figure 1.25:

FIGURE 1.25

The path of the **Sample.3dxml** file gets added to the **Discovery** dialog box (**Figure 1.26**).

10. *Click* the **OK** button to close the **Discovery** dialog box, as shown in Figure 1.26:

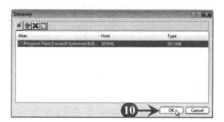

FIGURE 1.26

The path of the **Sample.3dxml** file gets added to the **Connect** dialog box (**Figure 1.27**).

11. *Click* the **OK** button to close the **Connect** dialog box, as shown in Figure 1.27:

FIGURE 1.27

The **Sample.3dxml** file opens in the user interface of CATIA V6 with a message displaying at the top right corner of the screen indicating that the connection is successful, as shown in **Figure 1.28**:

FIGURE 1.28

We now learn how to start a workbench in CATIA V6.

1.4 STARTING A WORKBENCH IN CATIA V6

A workbench in CATIA is a design environment that consists of a set of tools to enable users to perform design tasks of a specific category. CATIA V6 provides a number of workbenches to perform various design tasks. Some examples of CATIA V6 workbenches are Sketcher, Part Design, Assembly Design, Wireframe and Surface Design, VPM Editor, RFLP Editor, and Material Editor. Workbenches are grouped into workbench categories. For example, Sketcher, Part Design, Assembly Design, Wireframe and Surface Design workbenches are kept under the Mechanical Design workbench category; and VPM Editor, RFLP Editor, and Material Editor workbenches are kept under the Infrastructure workbench category.

Perform the following steps to start a workbench in CATIA V6:

1. *Open* CATIA V6 (**Figure 1.29**). The **Sample.3dxml** file opens, by default.
2. *Select* **Start > Mechanical Design > Part Design** on the CATIA V6 user interface to start the Part Design workbench, as shown in Figure 1.29:

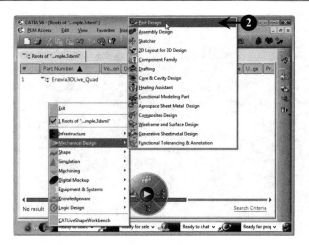

FIGURE 1.29

The **3D Shape/Representation DS** dialog box opens (**Figure 1.30**).

3. *Enter* a name for the representation in the **Representation Name** text box (Figure 1.30). In our case, we continue with the default name, **Representation1**.

4. *Click* the **Finish** button to close the **3D Shape/Representation DS** dialog box, as shown in Figure 1.30:

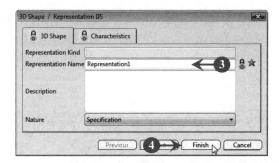

FIGURE 1.30

The **Part Design** workbench opens with the **Representation1** representation (**Figure 1.31**).

5. *Move* the mouse pointer over the button that displays the name of the current workbench, on the **Workbench** toolbar, to know which workbench you are working with, as shown in Figure 1.31:

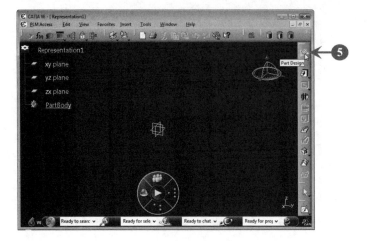

FIGURE 1.31

After learning how to start a workbench in CATIA V6, we now explore the CATIA V6 user interface.

1.5 EXPLORING THE CATIA V6 USER INTERFACE

CATIA V6 has an easy-to-use user interface that provides an enhanced design environment to work with 2D and 3D graphics. The CATIA V6 user interface contains a menu bar, various toolbars, and other components, such as specification tree and compass, to help you perform your design tasks. **Figure 1.32** shows the user interface of CATIA V6 when the **Part Design** workbench is enabled (the user interface may look slightly different if you have selected a different workbench):

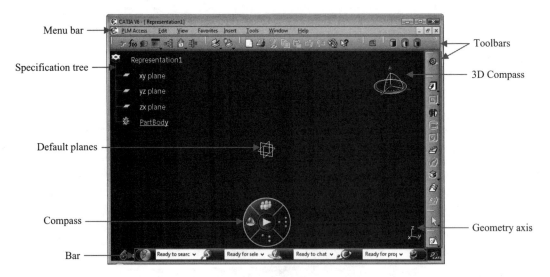

FIGURE 1.32

The various parts of the CATIA V6 user interface, shown in Figure 1.32, are as follows:

- Menu bar
- Toolbars
- Specification tree
- 3D Compass
- Compass
- Default planes
- Geometry axis
- Bar

We discuss each of these in detail.

Menu Bar

A menu bar is a collection of menus, each of which contains a set of options for performing various tasks. **Figure 1.33** shows the menu bar that is displayed on the CATIA V6 user interface when the **Part Design** workbench is enabled:

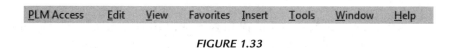

FIGURE 1.33

Each menu in the menu bar contains options for performing a specific category of tasks; for example, the **Edit** menu contains options, such as Cut, Copy, and Paste. The number of menus displayed on the menu bar depends on the currently active workbench. The menus that are common to all workbenches in CATIA V6 are PLM Access, Edit, View, Favorites, Insert, Tools, Window, and Help.

Toolbars

A toolbar works as a container for options that are used to perform various tasks while working on a CATIA V6 object. **Figure 1.34** shows a set of toolbars that appear below the menu bar on the CATIA V6 user interface:

FIGURE 1.34

Every workbench contains a specific set of toolbars; however, the Standard toolbar is present in all the workbenches.

Specification Tree

The specification tree monitors all the operations that are performed on the currently open CATIA V6 object. It appears on the top left side of the CATIA V6 user interface. You can use the specification tree to view or edit data. **Figure 1.35** shows the specification tree in the **Part Design** workbench:

FIGURE 1.35

Figure 1.35 shows that the **Representation1** node contains four sub-nodes: three default planes (*xy*, *yz*, and *zx*) and PartBody, which stores all the shapes and graphics drawn in a CATIA V6 object.

3D Compass

The 3D compass is displayed at the top right corner of the geometry area. It allows you to change the orientation of parts, assemblies, or sketches. Using the 3D compass, you can also change the orientation of the views of parts and assemblies. The 3D compass is displayed in **Figure 1.36**:

FIGURE 1.36

Compass

The compass is displayed at the bottom center of the CATIA V6 user interface. It serves the purpose of providing the user transparent access to PLM information at any time, on any object. The compass consists of five parts: four quadrants (North, West, South, and East) and the Play button. The Compass is shown in **Figure 1.37**:

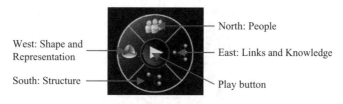

FIGURE 1.37

The function of each of the different parts of the Compass (Figure 1.37) is as follows:

- **North: People:** Allows you to access owner information.
- **West: Shape and Representation:** Allows you to access modification status information.
- **South: Structure:** Allows you to access structure information.
- **East: Links and Knowledge:** Allows you to access links and knowledge information.
- **Play button:** Allows you to play simulations.

Default Planes

By default, three planes are displayed at the center of the CATIA V6 user interface: xy-plane, yz-plane, and zx-plane. You can use any of these planes for drawing the sketch of a model (shape). The orientation of a model depends on its sketch; therefore, you should carefully select the sketching plane for drawing the sketch of the model. **Figure 1.38** shows the default planes:

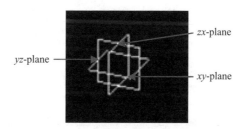

FIGURE 1.38

Geometry Axis

Being a 3D software, CATIA V6 follows a 3D-coordinate system, which has three axes: X, Y, and Z. Each of these axes represents a direction that is perpendicular to each of the other two axes. These axes represent the length, width, and height (depth) of an object. **Figure 1.39** shows the geometry axis:

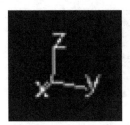

FIGURE 1.39

Bar

The bar is a strip containing the **Start** button and four domains: Search, Impact, Collaborate, and Propagate. It is present at the bottom of the CATIA V6 user interface. **Figure 1.40** displays different parts of the bar:

FIGURE 1.40

Clicking the **Start** button displays a menu containing different workbench categories from where you can select a workbench to work, as shown in **Figure 1.41**:

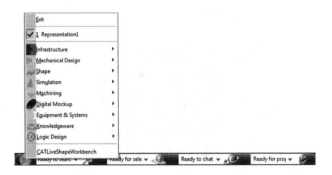

FIGURE 1.41

The menu that appears after clicking the **Start** button also displays the currently open CATIA V6 object. For example, the menu in Figure 1.41 displays **Representation1**.

Each of the four bar domains consists of two parts: a combo box on the left that allows you to enter the information and a button on the right that allows you to start the command (Search, Impact, Collaborate, or Propagate). The purpose of each of the bar domains is as follows:

- **Search domain:** Allows you to search objects by defining search criteria.
- **Impact domain:** Allows you to examine links and relations between objects.
- **Collaborate domain:** Enables instant collaboration between all participants across the extended enterprise to help them share data and ideas.
- **Propagate domain:** Allows you to propagate (that is, save) modifications made to objects to the ENOVIA database.

We now summarize the main topics covered in this chapter.

SUMMARY

In this chapter, you have learned about:

- New enhancements in CATIA V6
- Installation process of CATIA V6
- Opening process of CATIA V6
- Starting workbench in CATIA V6
- CATIA V6 user interface

Chapter **2**   # SKETCHER WORKBENCH

In This Chapter
◇ Invoking the Sketcher Workbench
◇ Drawing Shapes Using the Sketcher Workbench
◇ Editing and Modifying Sketches
◇ Working with Constraints on Sketches
◇ Summary

Computer Graphics-Aided Three-Dimensional Interactive Application (CATIA) provides an integrated environment called a workbench to create the design of sketches and solid models. The workbench consists of several options, such as the menu bar, Sketcher toolbar, and **Sketch** button that are used to create the design of an object. CATIA provides a number of workbenches that suit a particular design objective. They consist of all the functionalities required to create the designs in that workbench. For example, the Part Design workbench is used to create the solid model and the Sketcher workbench is used to draw basic sketches. For this purpose, the Sketcher workbench consists of various options for creating different types of shapes such as point, line, circle, and rectangle. Similarly, the Part Design workbench consists of the functionalities to create and modify the solid models such as sketch-bases and dress-up features.

In this chapter, we discuss the Sketcher workbench in detail, including the invoking of the Sketcher workbench and drawing of various shapes in the Sketcher workbench such as a line, circle, conic, profile, spline, and hexagon. Editing and modification of the existing shapes are also discussed in the chapter. Finally, applying and removing different types of constraints on the sketches are discussed in detail.

We begin the chapter with learning to invoke the Sketcher workbench.

2.1 INVOKING THE SKETCHER WORKBENCH

The Sketcher workbench is used to draw precise sketches and 2D shapes. Before working on designs of the sketches, it is essential to invoke the Sketcher workbench. Before invoking the Sketcher workbench, it is required to start the Part Design workbench (**Figure 2.1**).

Note: The steps for invoking the Part Design workbench are discussed in Chapter 1.

Perform the following steps to invoke the Sketcher workbench after starting the Part Design workbench:

1. *Open* CATIA V6 and *start* the Part Design workbench (Figure 2.1).
2. *Click* the **Sketch** (⊠) button in the **Sketcher** toolbar on the part design (Figure 2.1).

Note: Apart from the **Sketch** button the **Sketcher** toolbar also contains a **Positioned Sketch** button that is used to invoke a Sketcher workbench. We have invoked the Sketcher workbench by using **Sketch** button in the **Sketcher** toolbar.

3. *Click* on any one of the planes in the specification tree, according to which the Sketcher workbench invoked. In our case, we have *clicked* the **xy-plane**, as shown in Figure 2.1:

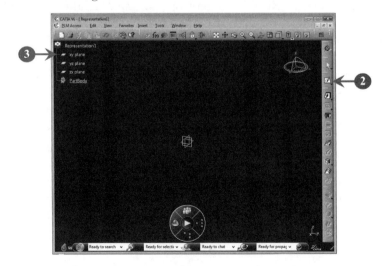

FIGURE 2.1

The *xy*-plane of the Sketcher workbench is displayed after invoking the Sketcher workbench, as shown in **Figure 2.2**:

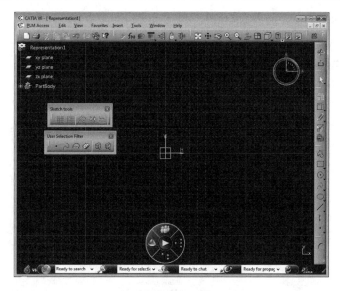

FIGURE 2.2

Figure 2.2 shows the Sketcher workbench that appears after selecting the *xy*-plane. We have closed the **Sketch tools** and **User Selection Filter** dialog boxes in the Sketcher workbench.

Before drawing the sketches, you can change the units and grid settings of the Sketcher workbench, if required. However, the settings facilitate the precise sketching of shapes in the Sketcher workbench. You can change the unit settings by opening the **Units** tab.

Perform the following steps to open the **Units** tab:

1. *Select* **Tools** > **Options**, as shown in **Figure 2.3**:

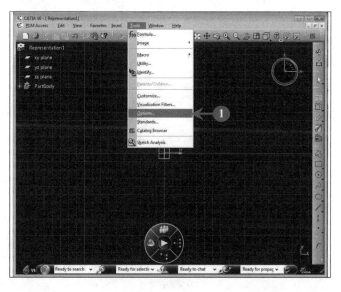

FIGURE 2.3

The **Options** dialog box opens (**Figure 2.4**).

2. *Select* the **Parameters and Measures** section that is displayed under the **General** node (Figure 2.4).

3. *Select* the **Units** tab, as shown in Figure 2.4:

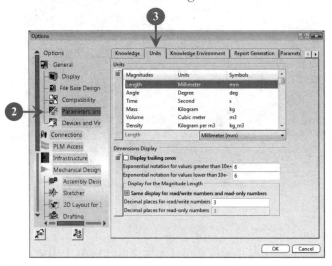

FIGURE 2.4

In Figure 2.4, you can change the desired settings for length, time, and volume. Apart from unit settings, you can also change the grid settings, by opening the **Sketcher** tab. Perform the following steps to open the **Sketcher** tab to change the grid settings.

4. *Select* the **Sketcher** option present under the **Mechanical Design** node. The **Sketcher** tab opens, as shown in **Figure 2.5**:

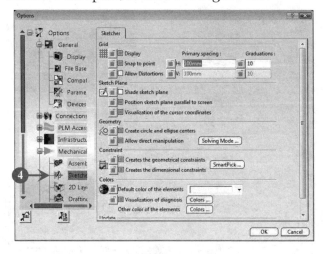

FIGURE 2.5

In the **Sketcher** tab, you can modify the following options:

- **Grid:** Helps to change the dimension of the grid, snap to point, and allow distortions.
- **Sketch Plane:** Helps to position the sketch plane parallel to the screen and visualization of the cursor coordinates.
- **Geometry:** Helps to create the additional elements in the geometry.
- **Constraint:** Helps to create geometrical shapes, such as circle and ellipse.
- **Colors:** Helps to specify the color of the drawing in the Sketcher workbench.

> **Note:** In this chapter, we set the graduation settings at 20 mm so that we can draw precise objects, such as a point, line, and rectangle.

We have learned how to invoke the Sketcher workbench and configure the settings of the **Units** and **Sketcher** options. We next learn to draw an object in the Sketcher workbench.

2.2 DRAWING SHAPES USING THE SKETCHER WORKBENCH

After invoking the Sketcher workbench, we can draw geometrical and other shapes in the Sketcher workbench. In this section, we learn to draw the following shapes on the Sketcher workbench:

- Point
- Line
- Rectangle
- Circle
- Profile
- Conic

We begin drawing shapes, starting with learning to draw points.

Drawing Points

A point is drawn on the basis of x and y coordinates. The point is the most common object drawn in the Sketcher workbench. The points in CATIA V6 can be drawn using different options. For example, you can draw a point without displaying its coordinates or a point whose coordinates are displayed. In addition, you can also represent a point on other geometrical shapes, such as a circle, line, or conic. In this section, we learn to draw points.

Drawing an Arbitrary Point

In the Sketcher workbench, you can create a point without providing the specific coordinates. In other words, an arbitrary point is located anywhere on the Sketcher workbench. You can create an arbitrary point by locating a position for that point anywhere in the Sketcher workbench. The final position of the point can be fixed by clicking the mouse at a desired location.

Perform the following steps to draw a point in the Sketcher workbench:

1. *Select* **Insert > Profile > Point > Point**, as shown in **Figure 2.6**:

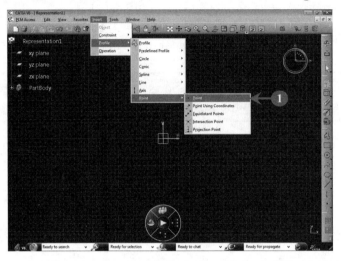

FIGURE 2.6

An arbitrary point and its coordinates (20, 20) are displayed on the Sketcher workbench, as shown in **Figure 2.7**:

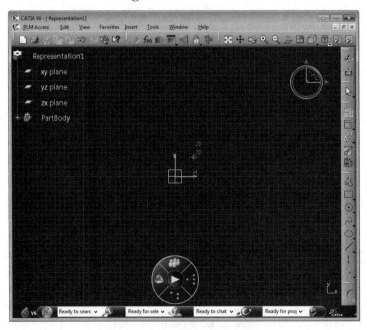

FIGURE 2.7

2. *Click* anywhere to fix a specific point in the Sketcher workbench. In our case, we specify the point at coordinate (30, 30) in the Sketcher workbench. The point is drawn successfully, as shown in **Figure 2.8**:

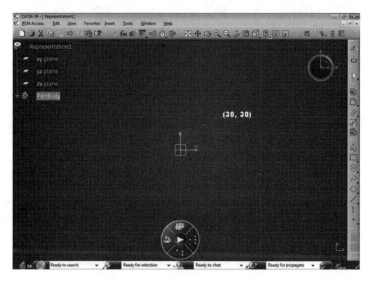

FIGURE 2.8

In Figure 2.8, a point at the coordinate position (30, 30) is shown on the *xy*-plane.

> **Note:** Instead of the default figure, additional details have been provided in the figure to improve the clarity for the reader.

Apart from this, you can also draw a point by using the coordinates. We next discuss how to create a point in the Sketcher workbench by using coordinates.

Drawing a Point Specifying Coordinates

The Point-Using Coordinate is a procedure that refers to the drawing of a point on the basis of the specific coordinates. In other words, prior to drawing a point, you need to provide its coordinates in the **Point Definition** dialog box. Moreover, the position of a point changes as per the change in the coordinates.

Perform the following steps to draw a point using particular coordinates in the Sketcher workbench:

1. *Select* **Insert > Profile > Point > Point Using Coordinates**, as shown in **Figure 2.9**:

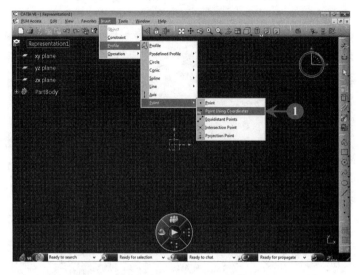

FIGURE 2.9

The **Point Definition** dialog box opens (**Figure 2.10**).

2. *Enter* the value for the horizontal position of the point, under the **Cartesian** tab, in the **Point Definition** dialog box. In our case, the horizontal distance is 30 mm.

3. *Enter* the value for the vertical position of the point, under the **Cartesian** tab in the **Point Definition** dialog box. In our case, the vertical distance is 30 mm.

4. *Click* the **OK** button, as shown in **Figure 2.10**:

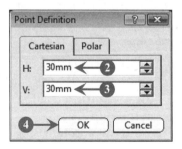

FIGURE 2.10

The point with the specified coordinates (30, 30) is drawn, as shown in **Figure 2.11**:

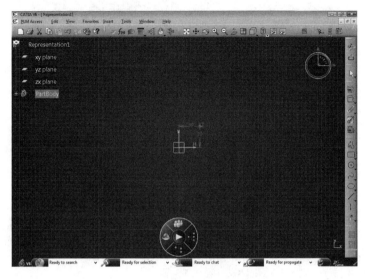

FIGURE 2.11

In Figure 2.11, a point with coordinates (30, 30) is shown.

After discussing how to draw a point, we next learn how to draw lines.

Drawing Lines

You can draw a line as well as an infinite line by using the **Insert** menu in the Sketcher workbench. In this section, we learn to draw the following types of lines:

- Lines
- Infinite Lines

Drawing a Line

You can sketch a line to draw a variety of shapes, such as a triangle, tangent, or parallelogram, in the Sketcher workbench. You can draw a line in the Sketcher workbench by first *clicking* on the starting point of the line, and then *dragging* the line to the desired length.

Perform the following steps to draw a line on the Sketcher workbench:

1. *Select* **Insert > Profile > Line > Line**, as shown in **Figure 2.12**:

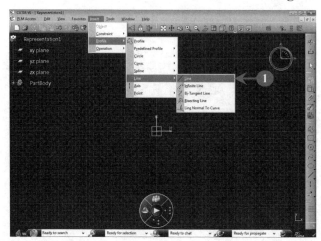

FIGURE 2.12

The starting point of a line and its coordinates are displayed in the Sketcher workbench, as shown in **Figure 2.13**:

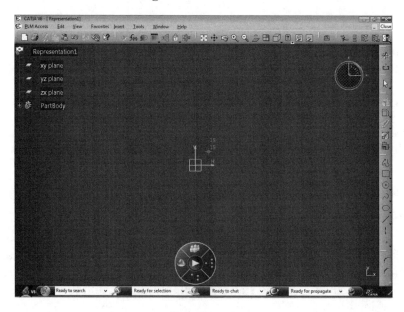

FIGURE 2.13

2. *Click* and *drag* the mouse pointer from the starting point coordinates to the end point of the line (up to where you want to limit the length of the line). In our case, the starting point coordinates of the line are (15, 15) and the end point coordinates are (100, 15), as shown in **Figure 2.14**:

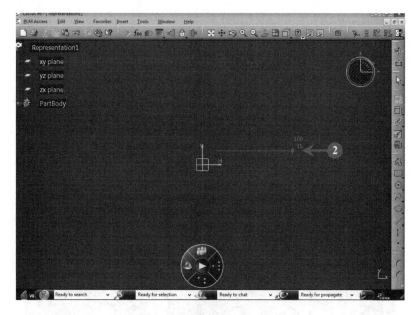

FIGURE 2.14

After fixing the starting and end points the final line is drawn, as shown in **Figure 2.15**:

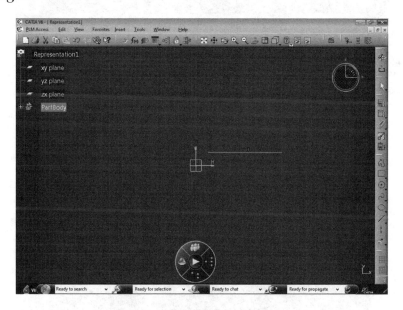

FIGURE 2.15

In Figure 2.15, a line with coordinates from (15, 15) to (100, 15) is drawn. After learning to draw a line, we next draw an infinite line.

Drawing an Infinite Line

An infinite line refers to a line in which the start and end points are not specified. These lines are generally used for advanced modeling of objects such as aircraft modeling.

Perform the following steps to draw an infinite line on the Sketcher workbench:

1. *Select* **Insert > Profile > Line > Infinite Line**, as shown in **Figure 2.16**:

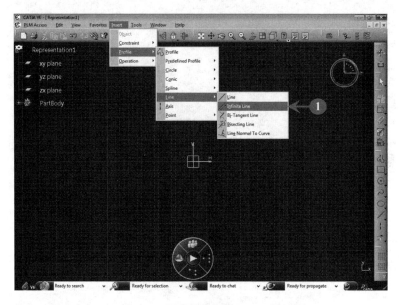

FIGURE 2.16

The coordinate (10, 40) specified by the user from which the infinite line is passing in the Sketcher workbench, is shown in **Figure 2.17**:

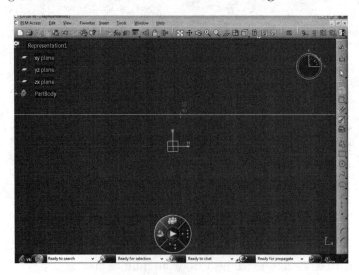

FIGURE 2.17

In Figure 2.17, the infinite line is displayed at coordinate position (10, 40).

2. *Specify* a position, then *drag* the mouse and *click* at the position where you want to set the infinite line. In our case, the infinite line is passing through coordinates (0, 0). Now, the final line is drawn, as shown in **Figure 2.18**:

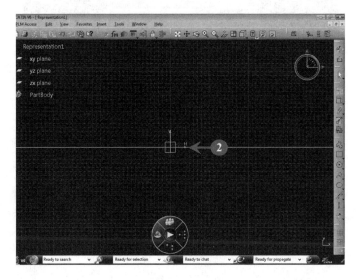

FIGURE 2.18

In Figure 2.18, an infinite line is shown that passes through coordinates (0, 0). After learning to draw an infinite line, we next learn how to draw rectangles.

Drawing Rectangles

The rectangles that are drawn in the Sketcher workbench can be a centered rectangle or an oriented rectangle. You can draw a rectangle in the Sketcher workbench by selecting the **Rectangle** option in the **Profiles** submenu under the **Insert** menu. However, in the centered rectangle, you first need to set the center of the rectangle before drawing the rectangle.

In this section, we learn how to:

- Draw a rectangle
- Draw a centered rectangle

Drawing a Rectangle

You can draw a rectangle anywhere in the Sketcher workbench.

Perform the following steps to draw a rectangle on the Sketcher workbench:

1. *Select* **Insert > Profile > Predefined Profile > Rectangle**, as shown in **Figure 2.19**:

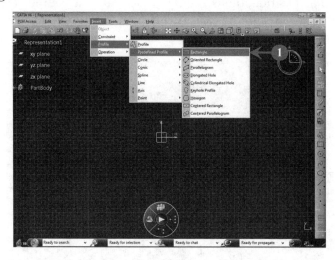

FIGURE 2.19

The Sketcher workbench is displayed with a point and coordinates, as shown in **Figure 2.20**:

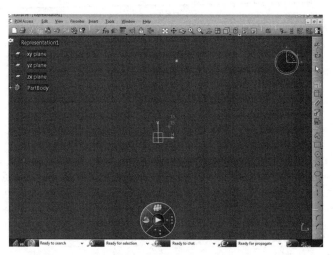

FIGURE 2.20

2. *Click* and *drag* the mouse pointer from coordinate (35, 35) to (110, 5). The final rectangle drawn is shown in **Figure 2.21**:

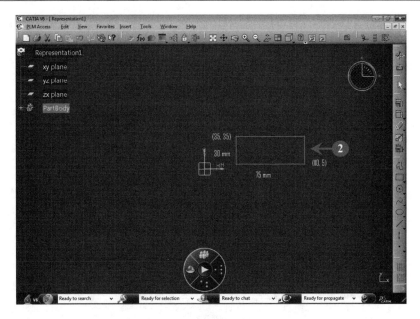

FIGURE 2.21

Figure 2.21 shows the rectangle with the specified dimension, where H (75 mm) denotes its horizontal dimension and V (30 mm) denotes its vertical dimension.

Note: Instead of the default figure, additional details have been provided in the figure to improve the clarity for the reader.

After learning to draw a simple rectangle, we now learn how to draw a centered rectangle.

Drawing a Centered Rectangle

The centered rectangle is a rectangle where the center of the rectangle is specified. You first select a point as the center and then draw the rectangle.

Perform the following steps to draw a rectangle with a center on the Sketcher workbench:

1. *Select* **Insert > Profile > Predefined Profile > Centered Rectangle**, as shown in **Figure 2.22**:

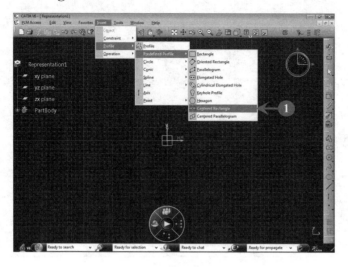

FIGURE 2.22

The Sketcher workbench is displayed with a point and the coordinates (**Figure 2.23**).

2. *Click* and *drag* the mouse pointer from a point with coordinates (20, 20) (center of the rectangle) to another point with coordinates (50, 20) that serves as the dimension of the rectangle. The final rectangle is drawn, as shown in **Figure 2.23**:

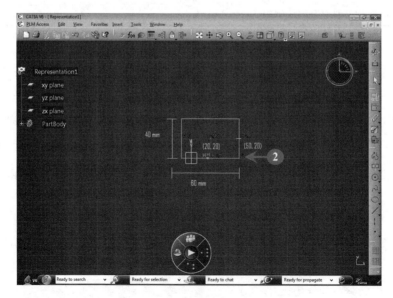

FIGURE 2.23

Figure 2.23 shows a rectangle drawn with a center at a point (20, 20) with the length and height of the rectangle as 60 mm and 40 mm, respectively.

> **Note:** Instead of the default figure, additional details have been provided in the figure to improve clarity for the reader.

Now, after learning to draw a centered rectangle, we learn to draw different types of circles.

Drawing Circles

The circle is an important and basic sketch from which various types of models are drawn. For example, to draw the model consisting of a wheel or a sphere, the drawing of a circle is necessary. In this section, you learn to:

- Draw a circle
- Draw a three-point circle
- Draw a circle using coordinates
- Draw an arc

Drawing a Circle

The center of the circle is specified when drawing a circle in the Sketcher workbench. The dimensions of the circle changes as per the movement of the mouse pointer from the center.

Perform the following steps to draw a circle on the Sketcher workbench:

1. *Select* **Insert > Profile > Circle > Circle**, as shown in **Figure 2.24**:

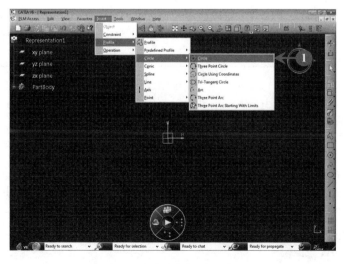

FIGURE 2.24

The Sketcher workbench is displayed with a point and the coordinates (**Figure 2.25**).

2. *Click* and *drag* the mouse pointer starting from the coordinate (20, 20), which serves as the center of the circle, to a point (80, 20) to limit the circumference of the circle. The final circle is drawn, as shown in Figure 2.25:

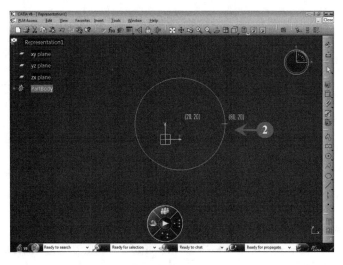

FIGURE 2.25

Figure 2.25 shows a circle drawn with a center at the point (20, 20) and a radius of 60 mm.

Note: Instead of the default figure, additional details have been provided in the figure to improve clarity for the reader.

Now, the procedure to draw a simple circle is complete. Next, we learn how to draw a three-point circle.

Drawing a Three-Point Circle

The three-point circle is a type of circle that passes through three points that specify the orientation of the circle in the Sketcher workbench. Perform the following steps to draw a three-point circle on the Sketcher workbench:

1. *Select* **Insert > Profile > Circle > Three Point Circle**, as shown in **Figure 2.26**:

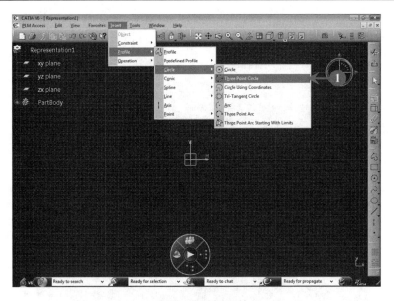

FIGURE 2.26

The Sketcher workbench is displayed with a coordinate that is displayed according to the mouse movement.

2. *Specify* the starting point for the three-point circle. In our case, this coordinate is (55, 35), as shown in **Figure 2.27**:

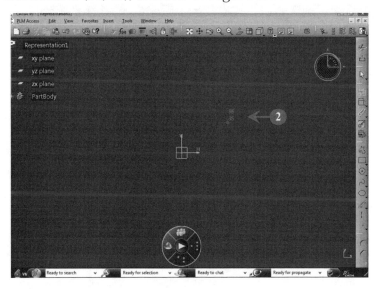

FIGURE 2.27

3. *Click* and *drag* the first point to the desired second point, through which the circle will pass. In our case, the line is dragged from the first point (55, 35) to

the second point (85, 35). The dotted line that appears from the first point to the
second point is known as the radius of the circle, as shown in **Figure 2.28**:

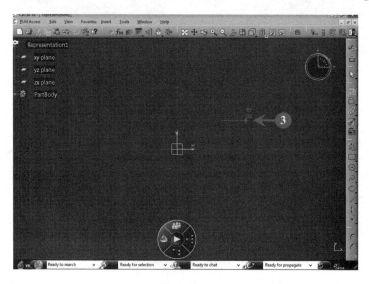

FIGURE 2.28

4. *Specify* the third point to complete the circle. In our case, we specified the
    third point at coordinate (70, 15), as shown in **Figure 2.29**:

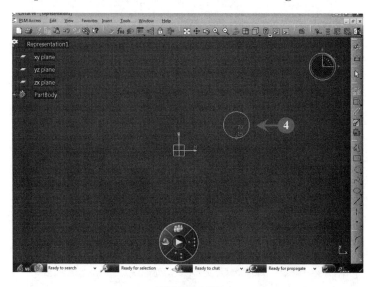

FIGURE 2.29

After specifying all three points the final circle is drawn, as shown in **Figure 2.30**:

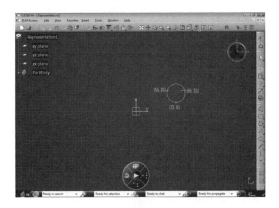

FIGURE 2.30

Figure 2.30 shows the final circle drawn by using the three points, (55, 35), (85, 35), and (70, 15), respectively.

Note: Instead of the default figure, additional details have been provided in the figure to improve clarity for the reader.

After drawing the three-point circle, we draw a circle using coordinates.

Drawing a Circle Using Coordinates

You can draw a circle using coordinates by specifying its coordinates and radius in the Sketcher workbench. The coordinates specify the position of the circle and the radius specifies its dimension (circumference) in the Sketcher workbench.

Perform the following steps to draw a circle using coordinates on the Sketcher workbench:

1. *Select* **Insert > Profile > Circle > Circle Using Coordinates**, as shown in **Figure 2.31**:

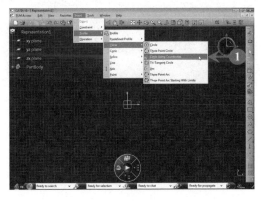

FIGURE 2.31

The **Circle Definition** dialog box opens (**Figure 2.32**).

2. *Enter* the horizontal and vertical distances as 50 mm, in the **Cartesian** tab of the **Circle Definition** dialog box.

3. *Enter* the radius as 20 mm in the **Circle Definition** dialog box.

4. *Click* the **OK** button, as shown in Figure 2.32:

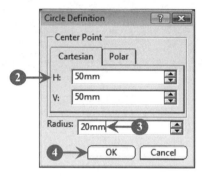

FIGURE 2.32

The **Circle Definition** dialog box is closed and the final circle is drawn, as shown in **Figure 2.33**:

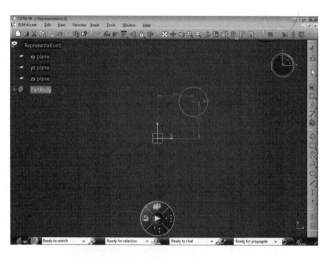

FIGURE 2.33

Figure 2.33 shows the final circle with horizontal and vertical distances as 50 mm, and radius as 20 mm.

After learning to draw a circle using coordinates, we next learn how to draw an arc.

Drawing an Arc

An arc is a part of a circle between two specified points. In this section, an arc with the center as (30, 30) and points (40, 40) and (40, 20) is drawn. Perform the following steps to draw an arc using coordinates in the Sketcher workbench:

1. *Select* **Insert > Profile > Circle > Arc**, as shown in **Figure 2.34**:

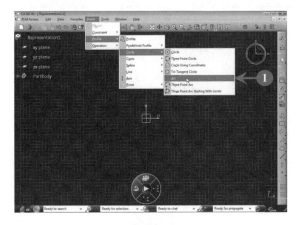

FIGURE 2.34

An arbitrary point set by user at (30, 30) is displayed (**Figure 2.35**). This point in the Sketcher workbench works as the center of the arc.

2. *Move* the mouse pointer from the first point (30, 30) to a second point (40, 40) through which the circle will pass (Figure 2.35).

3. *Move* the mouse pointer from the second point (40, 40) to the third point (40, 20) to complete the arc formation, as shown in Figure 2.35:

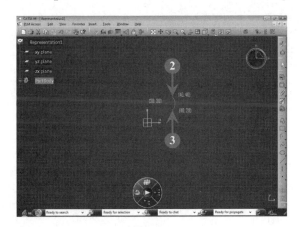

FIGURE 2.35

In Figure 2.35, an arc with center (30, 30), starting point (40, 40), and end point (40, 20) is displayed.

Note: Instead of the default figure, additional details have been provided in the figure to improve clarity for the reader.

After learning to draw all the shapes related to a circle, we now learn how to draw profiles.

Drawing Profiles

The profile is a shape that is formed by continuous lines or arcs. In this section, a profile consisting of three lines is drawn. Perform the following steps to draw a profile in the Sketcher workbench:

1. *Select* **Insert > Profile > Profile**, as shown in **Figure 2.36**:

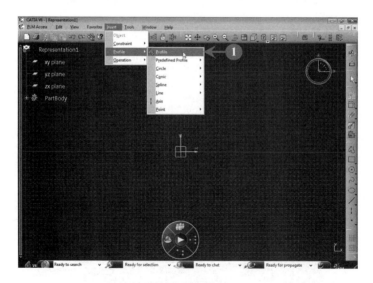

FIGURE 2.36

A point is displayed according to the movement of the mouse pointer, which is set at the point (30, 30) by clicking the mouse pointer at that position (**Figure 2.37**). This point in the Sketcher workbench serves as the starting point of the profile.

2. *Click* and *drag* the mouse pointer from the first point (30, 30) to another point (60, 60), as shown in Figure 2.37:

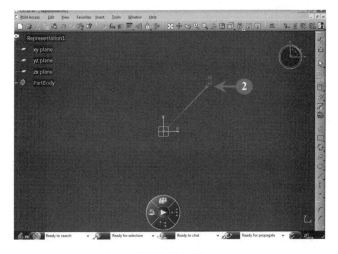

FIGURE 2.37

3. *Draw* the other lines in a profile, such as a second line from position (60, 60) to (30, 60) and a third line from position (30, 60) to (30, 30). The final profile drawn is displayed in **Figure 2.38**:

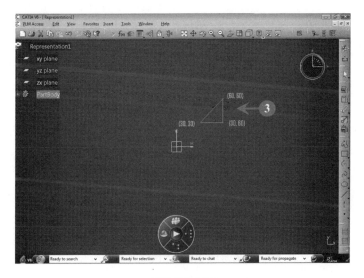

FIGURE 2.38

In Figure 2.38, a profile with three lines is drawn. The length of the first line is from point (30, 30) to (60, 60). The second line is drawn from (60, 60) to (30, 60). And the last line is drawn from (30, 60) to (30, 30).

After learning to draw a profile, we next draw various shapes associated with conics.

Drawing Conics

The conic is a geometrical shape that is drawn by cutting the various cross sections of a cone. For example, you can form a circle, ellipse, parabola, and hyperbola from a conic, as shown in **Figure 2.39:**

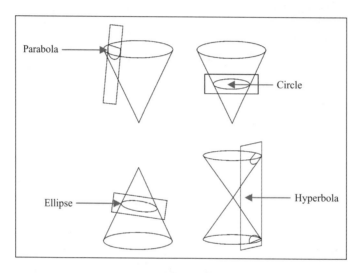

FIGURE 2.39

Figure 2.39 shows the different types of conics that are formed by cutting the various sections of a cone. In the following sections, you learn to draw the following conics:

- Drawing an ellipse
- Drawing a parabola by focus

Now, we learn to draw an ellipse in the Sketcher workbench.

Drawing an Ellipse

An ellipse is a geometrical shape that is formed by cutting a conic with a plane. In this section, we learn to draw an ellipse with the center as the origin (0, 0). Perform the following steps to draw an ellipse in the Sketcher workbench:

1. *Select* **Insert>Profile>Conic>Ellipse**, as shown in **Figure 2.40:**

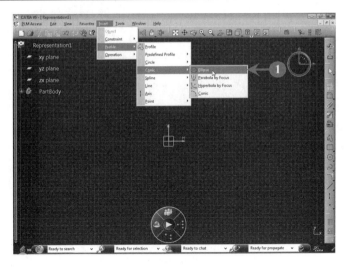

FIGURE 2.40

2. *Specify* the center of the ellipse by *clicking* the mouse pointer. In our case, we specify the center at coordinate (0, 0). This point in the Sketcher workbench serves as the center of the ellipse (**Figure 2.41**).

3. *Drag* the cursor from the center to the second point. In our case, the center is at coordinate (0, 0) and the second point is at coordinate (70, 0). The second point determines the orientation of the ellipse, as shown in Figure 2.41:

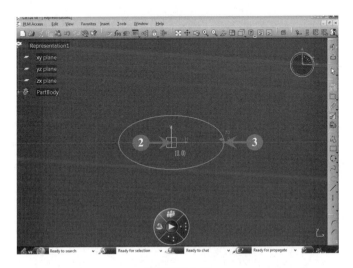

FIGURE 2.41

4. *Specify* the third point (50, 30) on the ellipse to determine the minor axis of the ellipse (**Figure 2.42**). The figure of the ellipse after all the parameters (i.e., center, focus, and axes) are set is shown in Figure 2.42:

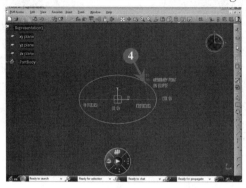

FIGURE 2.42

Figure 2.42 shows the various components of an ellipse; namely, the center, foci, major axis, minor axis, and point of orientation.

> **Note:** Instead of the default figure, additional details have been provided in the figure to improve clarity for the reader.

The final ellipse after clicking the mouse pointer on the position (50, 30) is shown in **Figure 2.43**:

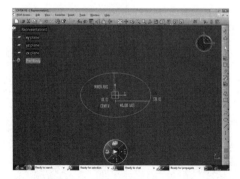

FIGURE 2.43

Figure 2.43 shows the final ellipse with the center at origin (0, 0).

> **Note:** Instead of the default figure, additional details have been provided in the figure to improve clarity for the reader.

After learning to draw an ellipse, we next draw a parabola by focus.

Drawing a Parabola by Focus

A parabola is also formed by a section of a conic (**Figure 2.44**). Parabola by focus is drawn by first locating its focus and then locating its vertex to finalize its orientation. Perform the following steps to draw a conic in the Sketcher workbench:

1.   *Select* **Insert>Profile>Conic>Parabola by Focus**, as shown in Figure 2.44:

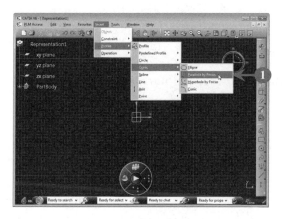

FIGURE 2.44

2.   *Specify* a coordinate that serves as the focus of the parabola. In our case, the coordinate is specified at (20, 0) in the Sketcher workbench (**Figure 2.45**).

3.   *Draw* the parabola through the point (0, 0), as shown in Figure 2.45:

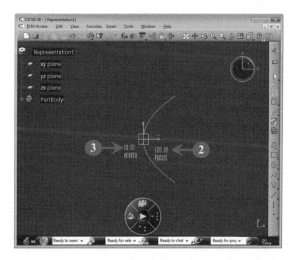

FIGURE 2.45

The parabola having a vertex at origin (0, 0) is displayed.

Note: Instead of the default figure, additional details have been provided in the figure to improve clarity for the reader.

We have learned to draw sketches of several shapes in the Sketcher workbench, such as a point, line, circle, and conic, after invoking the Sketcher workbench. Apart from creating the different types of shapes, you can also modify these sketches. CATIA V6 provides facilities to edit and modify these sketches by using various methods, such as trimming, chamfering, cornering, and mirroring. In the following section, we learn to edit and modify existing sketches.

2.3 EDITING AND MODIFYING SKETCHES

As is known, the Sketcher workbench provides the facility to draw various types of sketches in CATIA. In addition to drawing different shapes, it also provides the facility to edit these shapes (which have been previously drawn) in the Sketcher workbench. For example, if a rectangle is already drawn in the Sketcher workbench, then we can either trim any one of the sides or quick trim the entire sketch at any point of time. A user can perform the following activities for editing sketches:

- Trimming
- Quick Trimming
- Extending
- Cornering
- Chamfering
- Mirroring
- Rotating
- Scaling

We start by editing and modifying a sketch with the trimming operations that is used to remove either a part of or the entire sketch.

Trimming a Sketch

The Sketcher workbench provides the **Trim** tool that helps remove either unwanted sections or intersected portions of a sketch. For example, let's assume that there are two intersecting circles on which we intend to perform the trim operation.

Perform the following steps to trim the sketch:

1. *Select* the part of the sketch that you want to trim. In our case, we have selected a section of intersecting circles, as shown in **Figure 2.46**:

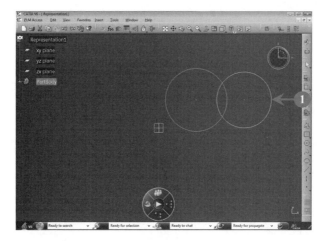

FIGURE 2.46

2. *Select* **Insert**>**Operation**>**Relimitations**>**Trim** to start the trim operation, as shown in **Figure 2.47**:

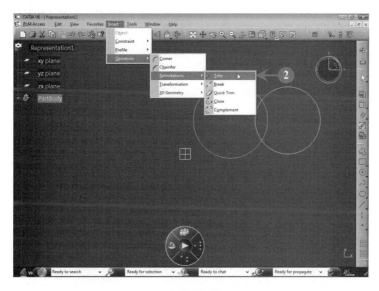

FIGURE 2.47

3. *Move* the mouse pointer and click to the selected part of the sketch (**Figure 2.48**). The selected part of the sketch is trimmed, as shown in Figure 2.48:

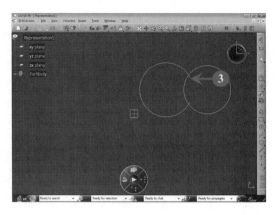

FIGURE 2.48

In Figure 2.48, it is seen that the selected part of the sketch is trimmed. After performing the trimming operation, we next learn the quick-trimming feature.

Quick Trimming a Sketch

CATIA also provides the feature of quick trimming a sketch. The **Quick Trim** option helps you to speedily trim the entire sketch. It is different from the trim operation that removes only a selected part of the sketch.

Perform the following steps to quick trim a sketch:

1. *Select* the part of the sketch that you want to trim. In our case, we select a section of the intersecting circles, as shown in **Figure 2.49**:

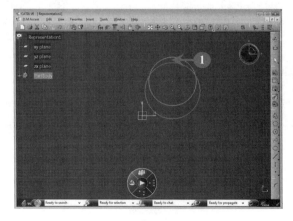

FIGURE 2.49

2. *Select* **Insert > Operation > Relimitations > Quick Trim** to start the **Quick Trim** operation, as shown in **Figure 2.50**:

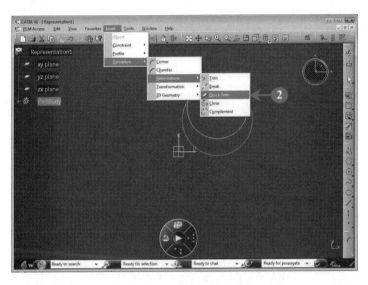

FIGURE 2.50

3. *Click* on the selected part of the sketch that is to be quick trimmed (Figure 2.49). The quick-trimmed sketch appears, as shown in **Figure 2.51**:

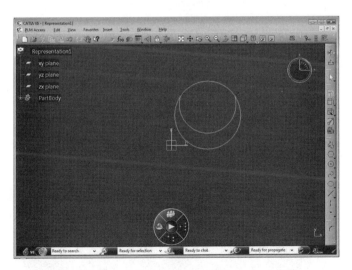

FIGURE 2.51

In Figure 2.51, the selected part of the sketch is quick trimmed.

After learning to quick trim a sketch, we next learn how to extend a sketch.

Extending a Sketch

A sketch is extended whenever one part of the sketch is connected, aligned, or stretched to another part. For example, you can connect a line to a circle or connect two different lines by extending a sketch. Perform the following steps to extend a sketch:

1. *Select* the line that you want to extend, as shown in **Figure 2.52**:

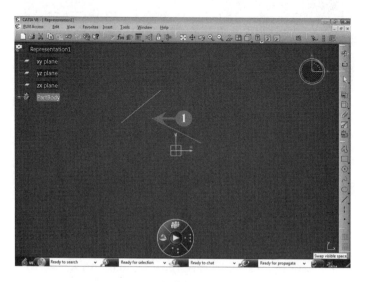

FIGURE 2.52

2. *Click* and *drag* the tip of the selected line (Figure 2.52). The line is extended, as shown in **Figure 2.53**:

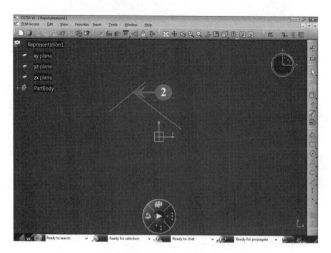

FIGURE 2.53

In Figure 2.53, the selected part of the line is extended in such a manner that the extended line is perpendicular to the other line. After learning the extending operation, we next learn how to corner a sketch.

Cornering a Sketch

The **Corner** option is used to create a smooth corner at the intersection of two lines. In other words, the cornering operation is used to smooth the sharp edges of a sketch.

Perform the following steps to corner a sketch:

1. *Select* the sketch that you want to corner. In our case, two intersecting lines have been drawn, as shown in **Figure 2.54**:

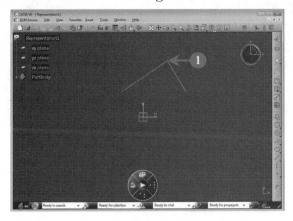

FIGURE 2.54

2. *Select* **Insert > Operation > Corner** to start the cornering operation, as shown in **Figure 2.55**:

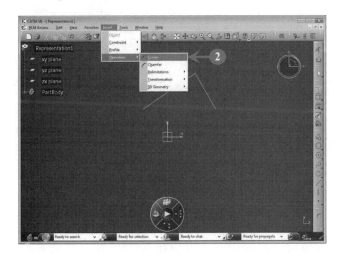

FIGURE 2.55

3. *Click* and *drag* the intersecting point of the lines. The cornered sketch is shown in **Figure 2.56**:

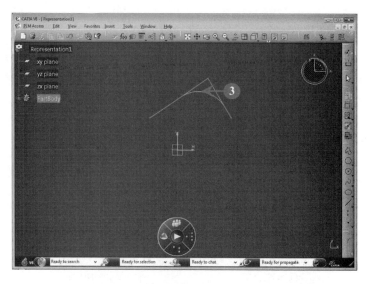

FIGURE 2.56

The final cornered sketch is shown in **Figure 2.57**:

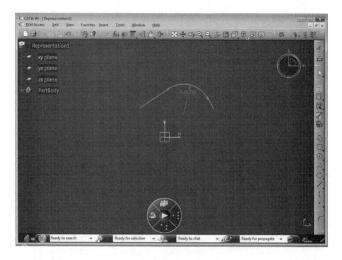

FIGURE 2.57

Figure 2.57 shows the cornered sketch with the curve of a radius as R, having length of 40.281 mm. The curve is created, after cornering the original sketch. We next learn about the chamfering of sketches.

Chamfering a Sketch

CATIA V6 provides the facility to chamfer the sketches by using the **Chamfer** option. The chamfering operation is used to chamfer sketches at a desired distance from the point of intersection in the Sketcher workbench. In the case of designing the mechanical components, the chamfer operation is done on the original sketch.

Perform the following steps to chamfer a sketch:

1. *Select* **Insert > Operation > Chamfer** to start the chamfering operation, as shown in **Figure 2.58**:

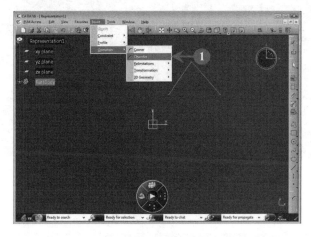

FIGURE 2.58

2. *Select* the intersection of the sketch that you want to chamfer. In our case, the intersection of the two lines has been selected, as shown in **Figure 2.59**:

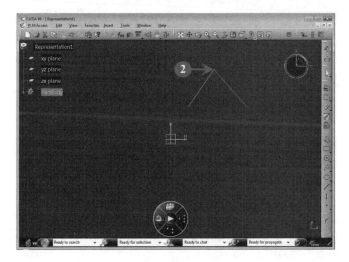

FIGURE 2.59

3. *Drag* the cursor from the intersection and *click* it at the desired distance to chamfer the sketch as shown in **Figure 2.60**:

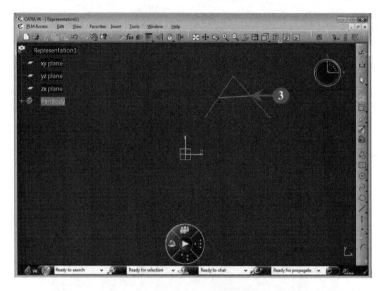

FIGURE 2.60

The final chamfered sketch is shown in **Figure 2.61**:

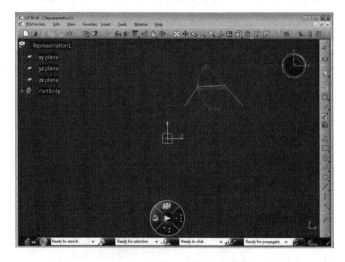

FIGURE 2.61

Figure 2.61 shows a final chamfered sketch with a length of 37.697 mm and at an angle of 51.51 degrees from the initial sketch. After chamfering a sketch, we next learn how to mirror a sketch.

Mirroring a Sketch

CATIA V6 provides the facility to mirror a sketch. The mirroring operation is done by using the **Mirror** option of the Sketcher workbench. The mirroring operation is used to form a symmetrical image of the initial sketch.

Perform the following steps for mirroring a sketch:

1. *Select* the diameter of the semicircle (which is the sketch to be mirrored), as shown in **Figure 2.62**:

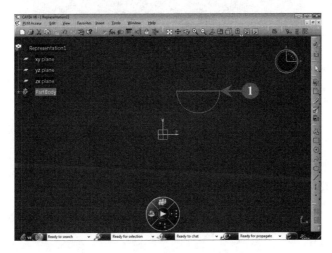

FIGURE 2.62

2. *Select* **Insert > Operation > Transformation > Mirror** to start the mirroring operation, as shown in **Figure 2.63**:

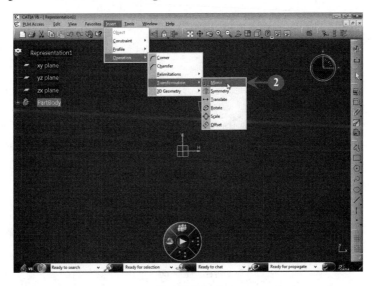

FIGURE 2.63

3. *Click* the diameter of the semicircle to set the alignment of the mirror image that is mirrored (**Figure 2.64**). After clicking, the semicircle mirror image is formed, as shown in Figure 2.64:

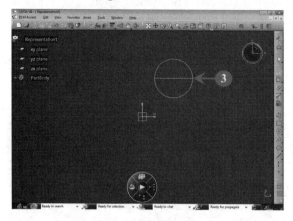

FIGURE 2.64

Figure 2.64 displays the final image that is a mirror image of the sketch (Figure 2.62).

After learning to mirror a sketch, we next learn how to rotate a sketch.

Rotating a Sketch

CATIA V6 provides the **Rotate** option to rotate a sketch at a specified point (rotate center point) by a desired angle. The most common use of the rotate operation is to model a wheel or other rotating components of a sketch by determining the direction and distance covered by the component in a single rotation.

Perform the following steps for rotating a sketch:

1. *Select* the line that you want to rotate, as shown in **Figure 2.65**:

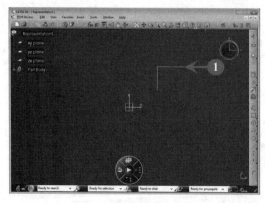

FIGURE 2.65

2. *Select* **Insert > Operation > Transformation > Rotate** to start the rotating operation, as shown in **Figure 2.66**:

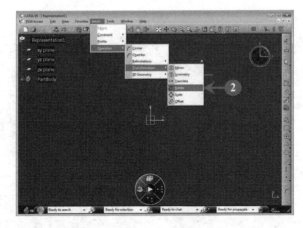

FIGURE 2.66

The **Rotation Definition** dialog box opens (**Figure 2.67**).

3. *Specify* the coordinate in the Sketcher workbench on the initial sketch along which the line is rotated (Figure 2.67). In our case, it is specified as (50, 70).

4. *Enter* the degree for the angle by which the sketch will be rotated in the **Rotation Definition** dialog box. In our case, the angle is 180 degrees (Figure 2.67).

5. *Click* the **OK** button, as shown in Figure 2.67:

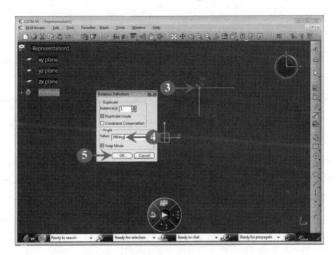

FIGURE 2.67

After clicking the **OK** button, the final rotated sketch is displayed, as shown in Figure 2.68:

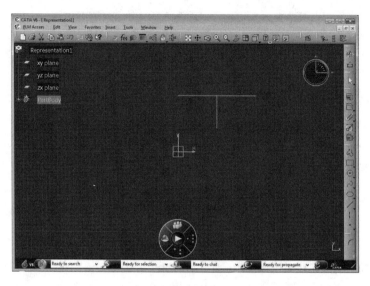

FIGURE 2.68

Figure 2.68 shows the final sketch rotated to an angle of **180** degrees at the coordinate (50, 70).

> **Note:** The rotated figure shown in Figure 2.68 displays the rotated as well as the selected part. In case you do not want to show the selected part of the sketch, clear the check box displaying the duplicate mode in the **Rotation Definition** dialog box.

After learning the rotation of sketches, we next learn how to scale these sketches.

Scaling a Sketch

The Sketcher workbench provides the **Scale** option to scale existing sketches. The scaling (also known as dilation) is a process used to compress or expand a sketch in either a vertical or horizontal direction. You can scale an entire sketch by resizing its dimensions. The scaling operation is commonly used in almost every sector of mechanical design to adjust the alignment of sketches.

Perform the following steps for scaling a sketch:

1. *Select* the sketch that you want to scale. In our case, we have selected all the
    sides of a rectangle, as shown in **Figure 2.69**:

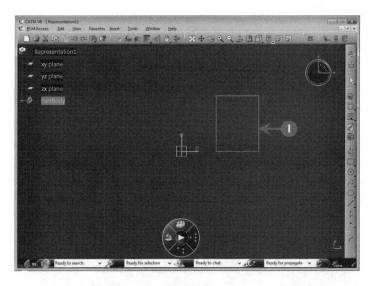

FIGURE 2.69

2. *Select* **Insert > Operation > Transformation > Scale** to start the scaling
    operation, as shown in **Figure 2.70**:

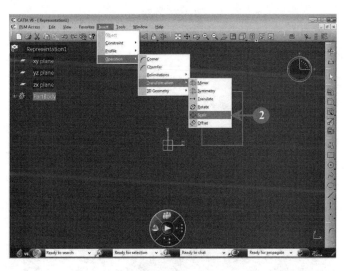

FIGURE 2.70

The **Scale Definition** dialog box opens (**Figure 2.71**).

3. *Select* the point at which the original image is scaled. In our case, the coordinate of the selected point of scaling is (45, 0) (Figure 2.71).

4. *Enter* the **Scale Value** in the **Scale Definition** dialog box. In our case, we enter 0.5 as the **Scale Value** (Figure 2.71).

5. *Click* the **OK** button, as shown in Figure 2.71:

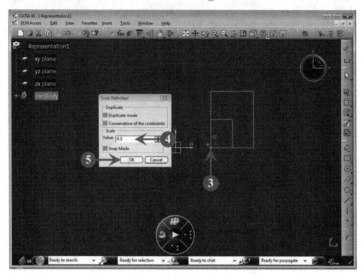

FIGURE 2.71

The final scaled sketch after specifying the parameter for the point and angle of rotation is shown in **Figure 2.72**:

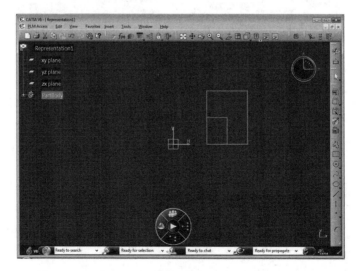

FIGURE 2.72

In Figure 2.72, the scaled sketch is drawn from the original sketch. The final sketch is positioned at point (45, 0) and is scaled to scale value of 0.5 of the original sketch.

Note: Instead of the default figure, additional details have been provided in the figure to improve clarity for the reader.

We have learned to modify the existing sketches in the Sketcher workbench, such as the mirroring, chamfering, and scaling operations. The sketches were drawn without imposing any constraints. In the next section, you learn to limit the shape as well as the orientation of the sketches by applying different types of constraints, such as geometrical, fix together, and contact.

2.4 WORKING WITH CONSTRAINTS ON SKETCHES

The constraints are applied to the sketches for limiting the properties and orientation of the sketches. They can be applied to modify the shape, size, and position of the sketch in the Sketcher workbench. In comparison to the editing modification, the constraints can also be added on the sketches. The primary difference is that after imposing the constraints, the sketches cannot be further modified or edited. We discuss, under the following heading, the common constraints that are applied to the sketches in CATIA V6:

- Applying a dimensional constraint
- Applying a contact constraint
- Applying a fix together constraint
- Applying the auto constraint
- Applying and removing multiple constraints

The constraints discussed here can be applied to the attributes of geometrical shapes, such as, in the case of a circle, the radius, center, or the diameter. *Select* **Insert>Constraints>Constraint Creation** from the menu bar to add the appropriate constraints to a particular sketch.

We start our discussion with applying geometrical constraints on sketches.

Applying a Dimensional Constraint

A dimensional constraint affects the position and dimension of a sketch in the Sketcher workbench. In other words, the dimensional constraints that are applied to geometric shapes limit the orientation of these geometric shapes. For example, geometrical constraints are applied to a circle to fix its radius and center; after application on the circle, its radius and center cannot be modified in the Sketcher workbench.

Perform the following steps for applying a geometrical constraint to a sketch:

1. *Select* the sketch to which you want to apply the dimensional constraints. In our case, we select a circle, as shown in **Figure 2.73**:

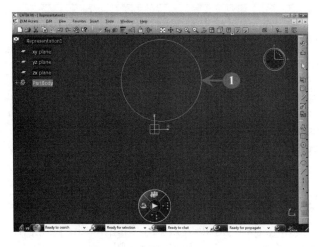

FIGURE 2.73

2. *Select* **Insert > Constraint > Constraint Creation > Constraint**, as shown in **Figure 2.74**:

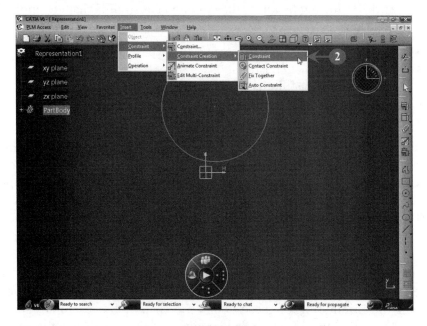

FIGURE 2.74

The workbench with dimensional constraint appears along with a constraint applied on the diameter by default (**Figure 2.75**).

3. *Click* the mouse pointer on the sketch where you want to apply the constraint, as shown in Figure 2.75:

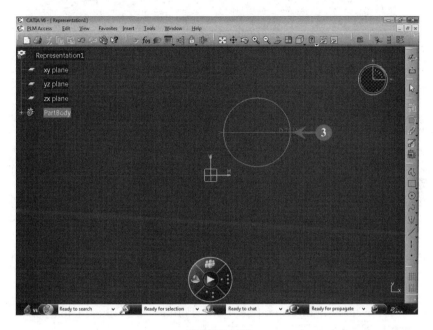

FIGURE 2.75

In Figure 2.75, the geometric or dimensional constraint is applied to a circle at a point D and the diameter of the circle is fixed as 72.111 mm. Now, if you *drag* the circle, you observe that you are unable to change the dimension of the circle, but only the position of the circle in the Sketcher workbench.

In the next section, we apply the contact constraint to a sketch.

Applying a Contact Constraint

The contact constraint is applied to modify the existing sketches in such a manner that they exhibit certain properties such as tangency, concentricity, and coincidence. For example, the contact constraint can be applied on two or more sketches to make them coincident, concentric, or tangent to each other.

Perform the following steps to apply a contact constraint to a circle to make it concentric to an ellipse:

1. *Select* the circle to which you want to apply the contact constraint (**Figure 2.76**).

2. *Select* **Insert>Constraint>Constraint Creation>Contact Constraint**, as shown in Figure 2.76:

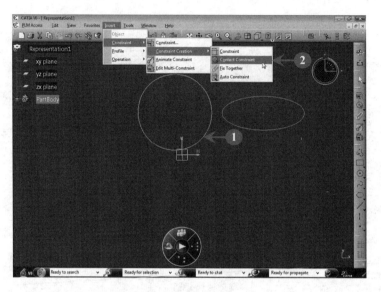

FIGURE 2.76

Now, after clicking on the circle, both sketches are concentric to each other, as shown in **Figure 2.77**:

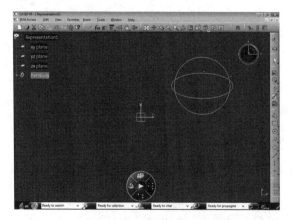

FIGURE 2.77

In Figure 2.77, the ellipse and circle are made concentric; that is, having the same center. Similarly, you can also create coincidence and tangency in sketches. After learning to apply the contract constraint to sketches, we next apply the fix together constraint to a sketch.

Applying a Fix Together Constraint

The fix together constraint attaches one sketch with another. The two sketches are fixed to each other such that they move together to any area in the Sketcher workbench.

Perform the following steps to apply the fix together constraint to a sketch:

1. *Select* two circles to which you want to apply the fix together constraint, as shown in **Figure 2.78**:

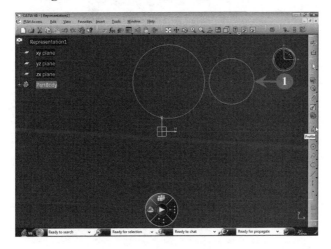

FIGURE 2.78

2. *Select* **Insert > Constraint > Constraint Creation > Fix Together**, as shown in **Figure 2.79**:

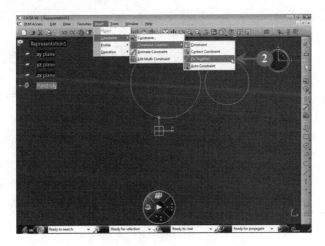

FIGURE 2.79

The **Fix Together Definition** dialog box opens, showing the points and circles with which the circle would be fixed (**Figure 2.80**).

3. *Click* the **OK** button in the **Fix Together Definition** dialog box, as shown in Figure 2.80:

FIGURE 2.80

The two circles are now fixed to each other, as shown in **Figure 2.81**:

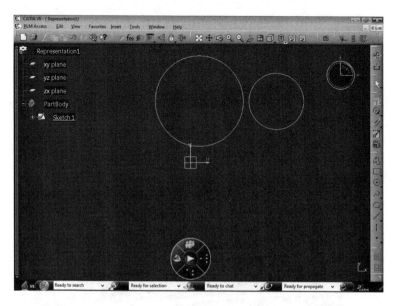

FIGURE 2.81

Figure 2.81 displays the fix together constraint that is applied to the two circles. Now, if you *drag* any of the circles, both circles will move together, as shown in **Figure 2.82**:

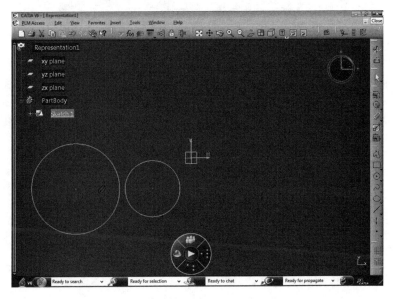

FIGURE 2.82

In Figure 2.82, the two circles on which the fix together constraint is applied move together from the original position. This implies that the circles are not attached visibly but by behavior.

After learning to apply the fix together constraint, we next learn how to apply auto constraints on the sketch.

Applying the Auto Constraint

All the possible constraints applicable on a particular sketch are applied after invoking the auto constraint. This is different from the rest of the constraints, where we need to apply each constraint individually, such as radius, length, and dimension.

In the Sketcher workbench, auto constraint is the option that when applied to any object will set all the possible constraints according to that object instead of applying each constraint separately.

Perform the following steps to apply an auto constraint to a sketch:

1. *Select* the sketch to which you want to apply the auto constraints. In our case, we have selected a line on which we need to apply auto constraints, as shown in **Figure 2.83**:

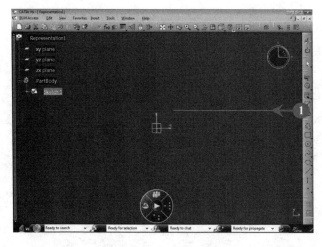

FIGURE 2.83

2. *Select* **Insert > Constraint > Constraint Creation > Auto Constraint**, as shown in **Figure 2.84**:

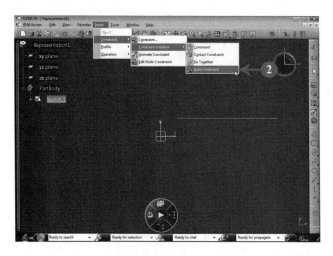

FIGURE 2.84

The **Auto Constraint** dialog box opens (**Figure 2.85**).

3. *Select* the sketch on which the auto constraint will be added. The selected sketch is added to the dialog box. In our case, we have selected the element to be constrained and 1 Line appears in the dialog box (Figure 2.85).

Note: 1 Line in the **Auto Constraint** dialog box denotes that only one line has been selected.

4. *Click* the **OK** button in the **Auto Constraint** dialog box, as shown in Figure 2.85:

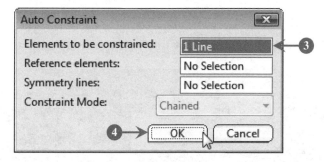

FIGURE 2.85

Now, the constraints for the line are applied, as shown in **Figure 2.86**:

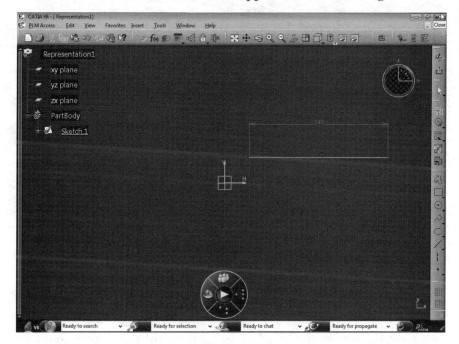

FIGURE 2.86

In Figure 2.86, the constraint added on the line is displayed after applying the auto constraint of length to it. Now, this line cannot be further modified.

Applying and Removing Multiple Constraints

We have learned to apply individual constraints to the sketches in the Sketcher workbench. Apart from applying individual constraints, you can also apply and remove multiple constraints. In other words, you can either apply or remove constraints to a particular sketch from the Sketcher workbench.

Perform the following steps to apply multiple constraints to a sketch:

1. *Select* the line to which you want to apply multiple constraints (**Figure 2.87**).
2. *Select* **Insert > Constraint > Constraint**, as shown in Figure 2.87:

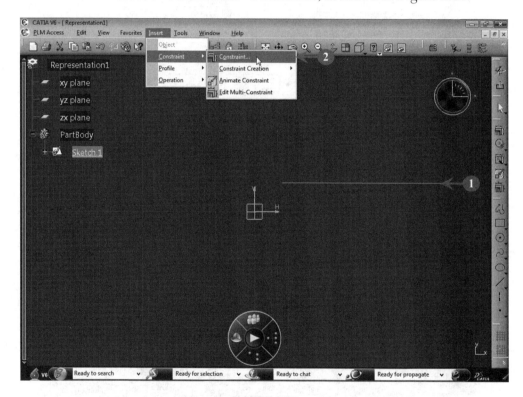

FIGURE 2.87

The **Constraint Definition** dialog box opens (**Figure 2.88**). The dialog box consists of a list of geometrical and dimensional constraints that are applied to a line along with the following constraints:

- **Length:** Applies the length constraints for the selected sketches
- **Fix:** Fixes the location of the constraints, such as fix the position of a line
- **Horizontal:** Fixes the horizontal constraint on the sketch

3. *Select* the **Length** and **Horizontal** check boxes to apply the length and horizontal constraints, respectively (Figure 2.88).

4.   *Click* the **OK** button, as shown in Figure 2.88:

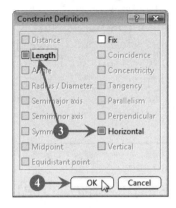

FIGURE 2.88

After applying the respective constraints, you see a figure similar to the figure displayed in Figure 2.87.

Apart from applying constraints, you can also remove a constraint using the **Constraint Definition** dialog box. This can be done by clearing the check box associated with the constraint, in the **Constraint Definition** dialog box. For example, if the check box containing the length constraint is cleared, then the length constraint is removed, as shown in **Figure 2.89**:

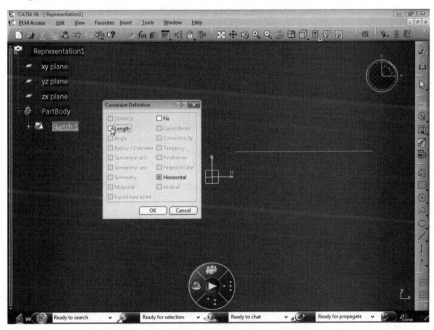

FIGURE 2.89

In Figure 2.89, the length constraint applied on the line is removed, as denoted by the focus on the length check box.

Now, the discussion on constraints ends. We have learned to add various constraints to the sketches apart from drawing and editing these sketches.

With this, you have reached the end of this chapter. We summarize all the topics covered in this chapter.

SUMMARY

In this chapter, you have learned about:

- The concept of invoking the Sketcher workbench
- Drawing shapes, such as a line, circle, and rectangle, in the Sketcher workbench
- Editing and modifying sketches by using the Sketch tools, such as trim and quick trim
- Applying constraints, such as geometrical, to the sketches along with the concept of applying and removing multiple constraints

Chapter **3**

PART DESIGN WORKBENCH

In This Chapter

◇ Using Sketch-Based Features
◇ Using Dress-Up Features
◇ Using Transformation Features
◇ Inserting Additional Bodies into Solid Models
◇ Summary

Part Design workbench is used to create solid models of the sketches drawn in the Sketcher workbench. Apart from creating solid models, the Part Design workbench is also used for advanced modeling of solid models, such as creating a hole, pocket, fillet, and adding rectangular as well as circular patterns. Moreover, the Part Design workbench is also used to modify the structure of a solid model by inserting an additional body into a solid model.

The Part Design workbench contains several options for advanced modeling of the solid models. For example, the sketch-based features are used to create solid models of the sketches that are drawn in the Sketcher workbench. Similarly, the dress-up features are used to modify the solid models created in the Part Design workbench. In addition, the transformation features are used to modify the solid models by transforming them along a direction, plane, or by symmetry.

In this chapter, we learn to create the solid models by using the sketch-based, dress-up, and transformation features of the Part Design workbench. We also discuss the addition of a body into a solid model.

We begin the chapter by understanding and using the sketch-based features of the Part Design workbench.

3.1 USING SKETCH-BASED FEATURES

The sketch-based features are used to create a solid model on the sketches that are designed in the Sketcher workbench. It is required to first draw the sketches in the Sketcher workbench and then create the solid model of these sketches in the Part Design workbench. Apart from creating solid models, you can also modify the solid models in various ways by creating holes, pockets, and shafts using sketch-based features.

In this section, we learn to use the following types of sketch-based features with solid models:

- The pad feature
- The shaft feature
- The pocket feature
- The hole feature
- The rib feature

We start by discussing the use of the pad feature to create a solid model.

The Pad Feature

The pad feature of the Part Design workbench is a feature that is commonly used to create a pad. A pad is created to add a solid base to a primary sketch that is drawn in the Sketcher workbench. In other words, you can use the pad feature to draw the solid models for sketches, such as a rectangle, parallelogram, or circle.

> **Note:** The default grid setting of the Sketcher workbench has been modified by changing the value of graduation settings as 20 mm. You can refer to Chapter 2 for procedures to change the graduation setting.

Perform the following steps to create a pad in the Part Design workbench:

1. *Create* a sketch by selecting **Insert > Profile > Predefined Profile > Hexagon** in the Sketcher workbench, as shown in **Figure 3.1**:

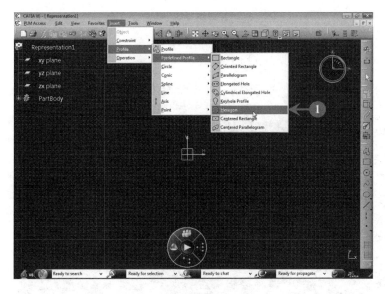

FIGURE 3.1

2. *Specify* the starting point at coordinate (55, 45), which serves as the center of the hexagon (**Figure 3.2**).

3. *Drag* and *click* at this point to coordinate (105, 45), as shown in Figure 3.2:

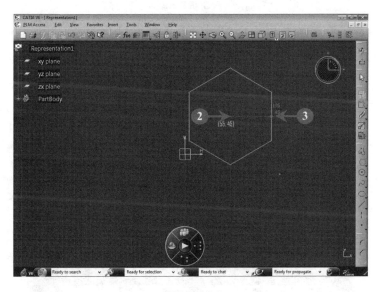

FIGURE 3.2

The final hexagon is created (**Figure 3.3**).

4. *Click* the **Exit workbench** button (⊞) in the toolbar of the Sketcher workbench, as shown in Figure 3.3:

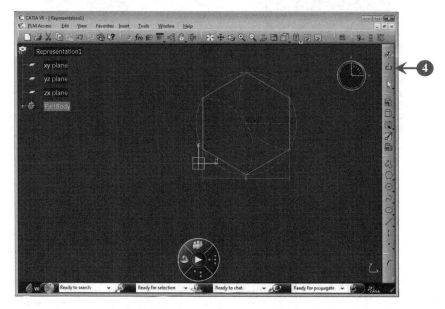

FIGURE 3.3

The sketch is displayed in the Part Design workbench, as shown in **Figure 3.4**:

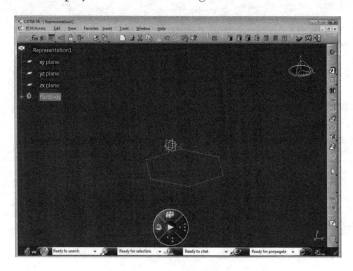

FIGURE 3.4

5. *Select* **Insert>Sketch-Based Features>Pad** in the Part Design workbench to select the pad feature, as shown in **Figure 3.5**:

FIGURE 3.5

The **Pad Definition** dialog box opens (**Figure 3.6**).

6. *Specify* the length of the solid model. In our case, we have specified the length as 30 mm (Figure 3.6).

7. *Click* the **OK** button in the **Pad Definition** dialog box, as shown in Figure 3.6:

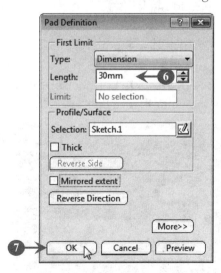

FIGURE 3.6

The solid model created is shown in **Figure 3.7**:

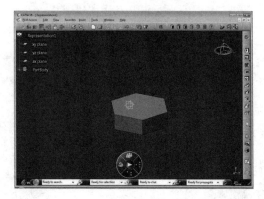

FIGURE 3.7

Figure 3.7 shows the solid model that was drawn by using the pad feature in the Part Design workbench.

We next learn how to use the shaft feature to create a revolved model.

The Shaft Feature

The shaft feature of the Part Design workbench is used to create a revolving solid model. The sketch drawn in the Sketcher workbench is revolved around a specific axis at a specified angle. You can find the correct estimation of the orientation and revolution of a particular sketch while creating a revolved solid model. This data can be used for further improvement of the solid model.

Perform the following steps to create a shaft:

1. *Create* a sketch in the Sketcher workbench. In our case, we have created a semicircle (**Figure 3.8**).
2. *Click* the **Exit workbench** button (⬚) in the toolbar of the Sketcher workbench, as shown in Figure 3.8:

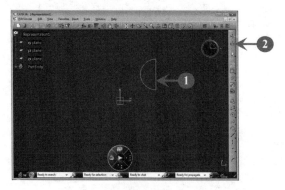

FIGURE 3.8

The sketch drawn is displayed in the Part Design workbench, as shown in
Figure 3.9:

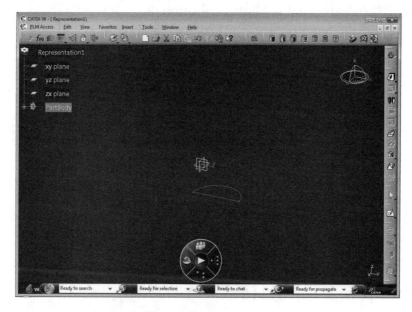

FIGURE 3.9

3. *Select* **Insert > Sketch-Based Features > Shaft** in the Part Design workbench
    to add the shaft feature, as shown in **Figure 3.10**:

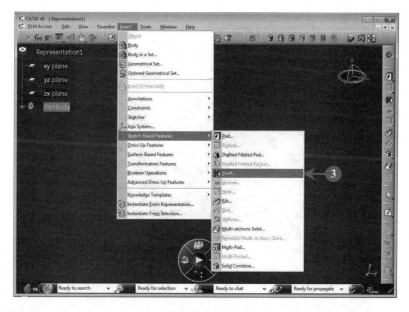

FIGURE 3.10

The **Shaft Definition** dialog box opens (**Figure 3.11**).

4. *Specify* the angle of rotation for the sketch. In our case, the first angle is set to 360 degrees in the **Shaft Definition** dialog box (Figure 3.11).

5. *Select* the **Selection** box in **Profile/Surface** group and select the sketch that is added in the **Selection** box. In our case, we select Sketch.6 (Figure 3.11).

6. *Select* the axis in the **Axis** option along which the image will be rotated (Figure 3.11).

7. *Click* the **OK** button in **Shaft Definition** dialog box, as shown in Figure 3.11:

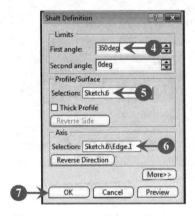

FIGURE 3.11

The final solid model after adding the shaft feature is shown in **Figure 3.12**:

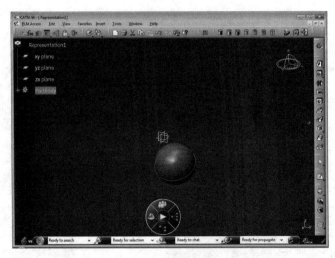

FIGURE 3.12

Figure 3.12 shows the revolved solid model using the shaft feature in the Part Design workbench. We next learn to use a pocket feature to remove a part from the solid model.

The Pocket Feature

The pocket feature of the Part Design workbench creates a pocket in the solid model by removing a selected portion from a solid model. The utility of the pocket feature is to form the resulting solid image by extruding different surfaces from a solid model. In other words, the utility of the pocket feature is the creation of a precise cut in the solid model to make a design or pattern with a cavity.

Perform the following steps to create a pocket:

1. *Create* a shape in the Sketcher workbench. In our case, we create a parallelogram (**Figure 3.13**).
2. *Click* the **Exit workbench** button ( ) in the toolbar of the Sketcher workbench, as shown in Figure 3.13:

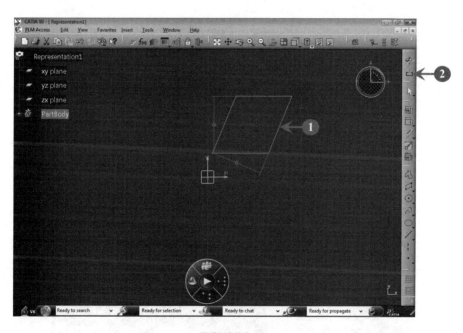

FIGURE 3.13

The sketch drawn in the Part Design workbench is shown in **Figure 3.14**:

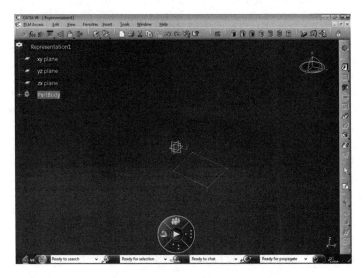

FIGURE 3.14

3. *Select* **Insert>Sketch-Based Features>Pad** in Part Design workbench to pad the sketch and display a preview model (Figure 3.5). The **Pad Definition** dialog box appears (**Figure 3.15**).

4. *Click* the **OK** button in the **Pad Definition** dialog box, as shown in Figure 3.15:

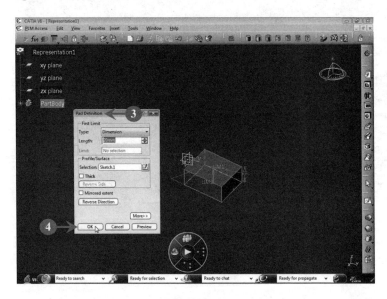

FIGURE 3.15

In our case, we use the default settings in the **Pad Definition** dialog box (Figure 3.15).

The solid model after adding the pad feature is shown in **Figure 3.16**:

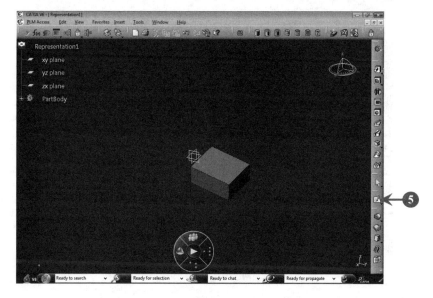

FIGURE 3.16

5. *Open* this solid model (Figure 3.16) in the Sketcher workbench by using the **Sketch** button (▨). A new image will pop up, as shown in **Figure 3.17**:

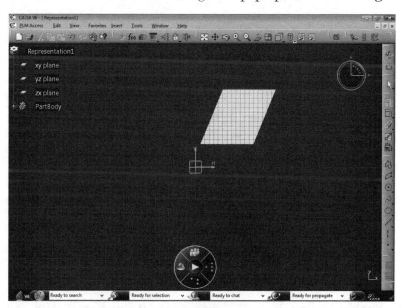

FIGURE 3.17

6. *Modify* the sketch (shown in Figure 3.17) to add the pocket feature. The final sketch is shown in **Figure 3.18**:

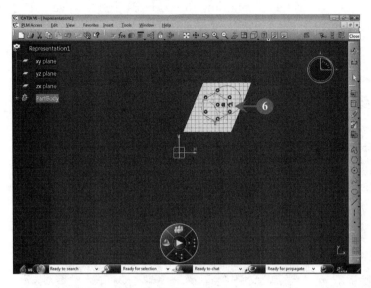

FIGURE 3.18

7. *Open* the sketch (Figure 3.18) in the Part Design workbench.
8. *Select* **Insert > Sketch-Based Features > Pocket** in Part Design workbench to select the pocket feature, as shown in **Figure 3.19**:

FIGURE 3.19

The **Pocket Definition** dialog box appears. It shows the default values for the pocket feature and preview in **Figure 3.20**:

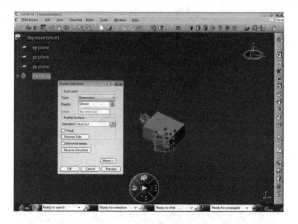

FIGURE 3.20

9. *Set* the **Type** option as **Up to last** limit to create a solid model by pushing out a fixed cross section of the hexagon or extruding it completely through the initial solid model (**Figure 3.21**).

Note: The **Pocket Definition** dialog box consists of **First Limit** sections that specify the several extensions of a pocket in the solid model, such as **Up to next, Up to last, Up to plane**. The **Up to last** option specifies that the pocket would completely extrude through the initial solid model. In other words, the extruding **Up to last** option would push out the complete surface of the solid model. The **Profile/Surface** section specifies the sketch that is added as a pocket.

10. *Select* the sketch that would be added as a pocket of the solid model. In our case it is **Sketch.2**. Now, *click* the **OK** button in the **Pocket Definition** dialog box, as shown in Figure 3.21:

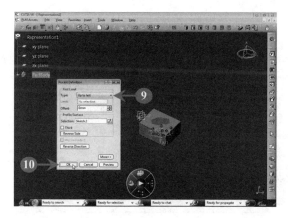

FIGURE 3.21

The final solid model, along with the pocket feature, is displayed in **Figure 3.22**:

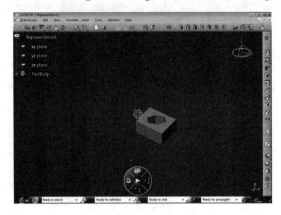

FIGURE 3.22

In Figure 3.22, a pocket is displayed that was created by cutting through the solid cross section (hexagon). The main utility of the pocket feature is to form a solid model by extruding different shapes, such as a circle, spline, ellipse, or rectangle.

After discussing the pocket feature, we next learn how to use the hole feature to create a hole in a solid model.

The Hole Feature

The hole feature of the Part Design workbench is used to create a hole in a solid model. You create a hole in a solid model to join two solid models.

Perform the following steps to create a hole in a solid model:

1. *Create* a cylindrical elongated hole in the Sketcher workbench (**Figure 3.23**).
2. *Click* the **Exit workbench** button (⬚) in the toolbar of the Sketcher workbench, as shown in Figure 3.23:

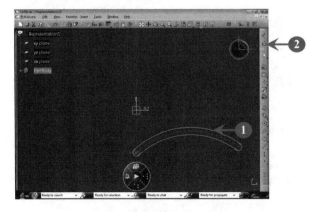

FIGURE 3.23

The sketch is displayed in the Part Design workbench, as shown in **Figure 3.24**:

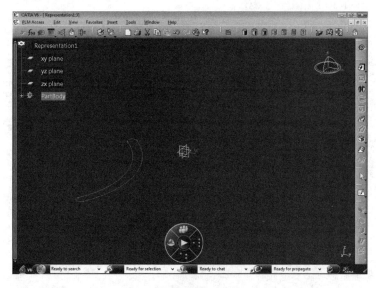

FIGURE 3.24

3. *Create* the solid model of the sketch by using the pad feature (Figure 3.5). The final model of the solid is shown in **Figure 3.25**:

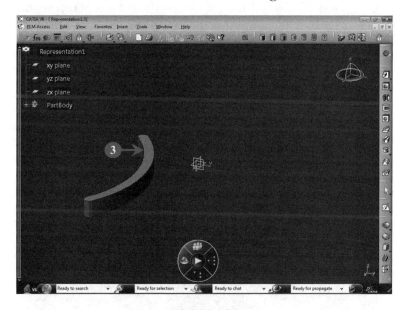

FIGURE 3.25

4. *Select* the hole feature using **Insert > Sketch-Based Features > Hole**, as shown in **Figure 3.26**:

FIGURE 3.26

Click at a point on a solid model to open the **Hole Definition** dialog box (**Figure 3.27**). It reflects the default values for the hole feature, as shown in Figure 3.27:

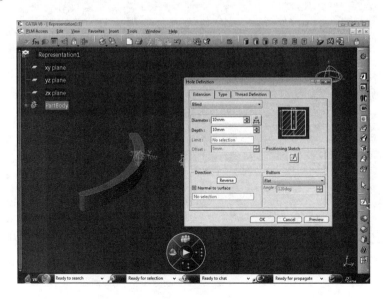

FIGURE 3.27

5. *Select* the **Up To Last** option from the drop-down list in the **Extension** tab, as shown in **Figure 3.28**:

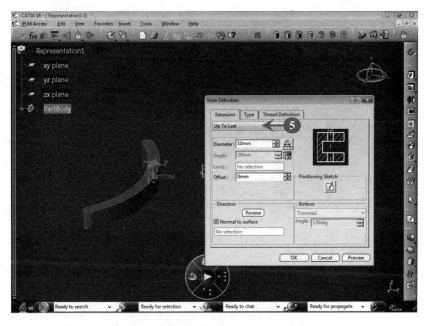

FIGURE 3.28

Note: The **Hole Definition** dialog box includes an Extension tab that specifies the several extensions of a hole in a solid model, such as **Blind, Up To Next, Up To Last**, and **Up To Plane**. The **Up To Last** option specifies that the hole would be added up to the last face of a solid model. In other words, the extruding **Up To Last** option would create a hole through the complete depth of the solid originating from the part of solid model that is selected.

6. *Select* the default settings in the **Type** tab that is **Simple**, as a simple hole is being created (**Figure 3.29**).

Note: The **Simple** option is selected as the default hole. Apart from selecting the default setting, you can also draw some other types of hole, such as **Tapered, Counterbored, Countersunk**, and **Counterdrilled** by selecting different options from the drop-down list under the **Type** tab in the **Hole Definition** dialog box.

7.   *Click* the **OK** button, as shown in Figure 3.29:

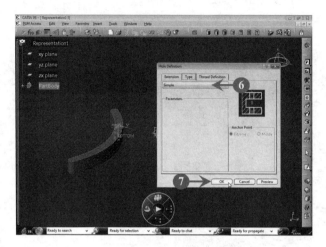

FIGURE 3.29

The final figure after inserting the **Simple** hole is shown in **Figure 3.30**:

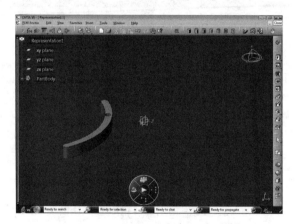

FIGURE 3.30

> **Note:** The pocket feature is different from a hole in the shape, as the shapes formed by the result of the two operations are different. A hole is circular in shape, whereas a pocket can be formed in any shape.

After discussing the hole feature, we next learn how to use the rib feature for advanced modeling of solid models.

The Rib Feature

The rib feature of the Part Design workbench is used to bend a profile along a curve. The curve and the profile are drawn in the Sketcher workbench and the rib feature is added in the Part Design workbench. In addition, the curve also acts as a reference along which the element (profile) is bent.

Perform the following steps to create a rib:

1. *Create* a curve on which the rib would be formed in the Sketcher workbench. In our case, we create a spline (**Figure 3.31**).

2. *Click* the **Exit workbench** button (⬛) in the toolbar of the Sketcher workbench, as shown in Figure 3.31:

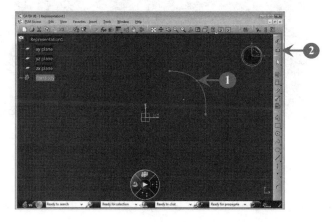

FIGURE 3.31

The sketch appears in the Part Design workbench, as shown in **Figure 3.32**:

FIGURE 3.32

3. *Exit* from the Part Design workbench by using the **Sketch** button of the **Sketcher** toolbar and open the curve (Figure 3.32) in the Sketcher workbench by selecting the **yz-plane** from the specification tree, as shown in **Figure 3.33**:

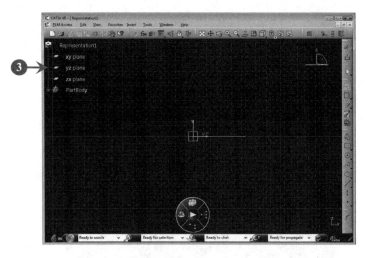

FIGURE 3.33

4. *Draw* a profile in the Sketcher workbench on which the rib feature is added. In our case, a parallelogram is sketched on the spline (**Figure 3.34**).

5. *Select* the **Exit workbench** button (⬛) from the Sketcher workbench, as shown in Figure 3.34:

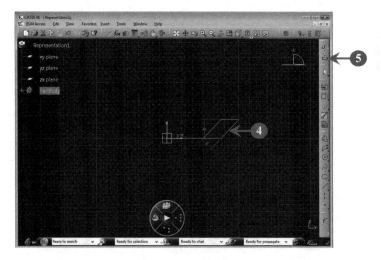

FIGURE 3.34

The preview of the curve and profile in the Part Design workbench is shown in **Figure 3.35**:

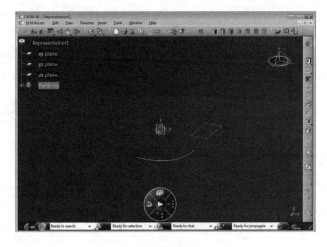

FIGURE 3.35

6. *Select* the rib feature by using **Insert > Sketch-Based Features > Rib**, as shown in **Figure 3.36**:

FIGURE 3.36

The **Rib Definition** dialog box is opened, as shown in **Figure 3.37**:

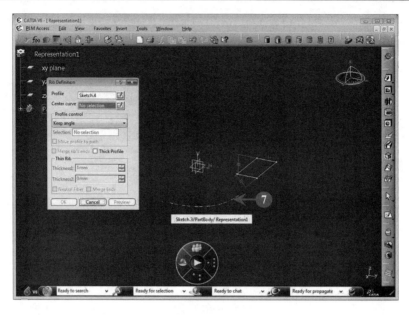

FIGURE 3.37

7. *Select* the profile curve to create a rib (Figure 3.37). The preview of the rib is displayed in **Figure 3.38**.

8. *Click* the **OK** button in the **Rib Definition** dialog box, as shown in Figure 3.38:

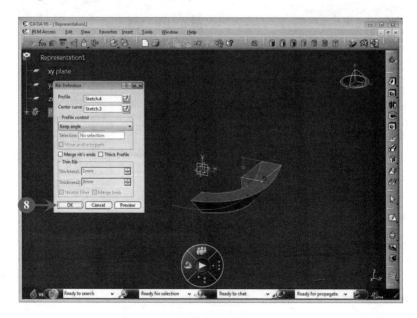

FIGURE 3.38

The final ribbed curve is created, as shown in **Figure 3.39**:

FIGURE 3.39

Figure 3.39 shows the final sketch after the rib feature is added.

Note: All the sketches cannot be added in the Sketcher workbench at an instance; therefore, to add the new part in a different plane, we need to first exit from the Sketcher workbench and reopen it in another plane. The following are the basic requirements that form the basis for transition between the Sketcher and Part Design workbenches:

1. When the requirement is to create a solid model of the sketch in the Part Design workbench using the pad feature and then add the additional sketch to the solid model, we need to switch from the Part Design workbench to the Sketcher workbench and add the additional features. An example is adding a pocket.
2. When the requirement is to create a sketch in the Sketcher workbench and modify it by adding a new sketch, we need to exit from the Sketcher workbench to the Part Design workbench and reopen the sketch in the Sketcher workbench. An example is creating a ribbed curve.

We have learned to add sketch-based features to the solid model including the pad, shaft, pocket, hole, and rib features. We next learn how to add the dress-up feature to the existing sketches in the Part Design workbench.

3.2 USING DRESS-UP FEATURES

The dress-up features, such as fillet, chamfer, draft, and shell, are added to the solid models in the Part Design workbench. While adding the dress-up features, you do not need to modify the initial sketch by drawing any additional sketches. You can directly apply the dress-up features on the solid model. In this section, we create solid models and add the following types of dress-up features:

- The fillet feature
- The chamfer feature
- The draft feature
- The shell feature

We start the discussion with the use of the fillet feature.

The Fillet Feature

The fillet feature is used to create a rounded corner at the intersection of two surfaces. In addition, if a surface is selected, then all the edges corresponding to that surface are filleted. CATIA V6 provides different types of fillets in the Part Design workbench, such as:

- The edge fillet feature
- The variable radius fillet feature
- The face–face fillet feature
- The tritangent fillet feature

The Edge Fillet Feature

The edge fillet feature is used to fillet or round the sharpened edges of a solid model. Perform the following steps to add an edge fillet and create the edge-filleted solid model:

1. *Create* a sketch in the Sketcher workbench. In our case, we create a hexagon (**Figure 3.40**).
2. *Select* the **Exit workbench** button (⊞) from the Sketcher workbench, as shown in Figure 3.40:

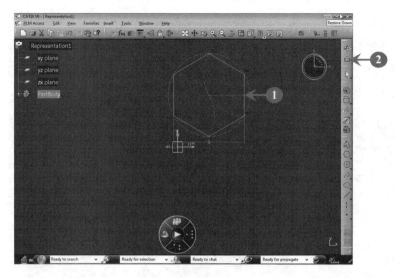

FIGURE 3.40

The sketch drawn is displayed in the Part Design workbench, as shown in **Figure 3.41**:

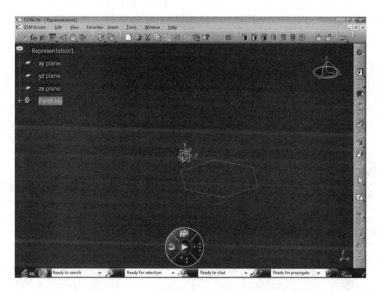

FIGURE 3.41

3. *Create* a solid model of the sketch by using the pad feature. The solid model created is shown in **Figure 3.42**:

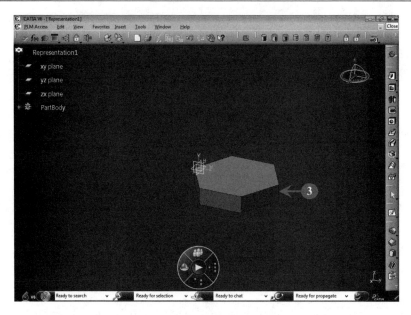

FIGURE 3.42

4. *Select* **Insert > Dress-Up Features > Edge Fillet** to select the edge fillet feature, as shown in **Figure 3.43**:

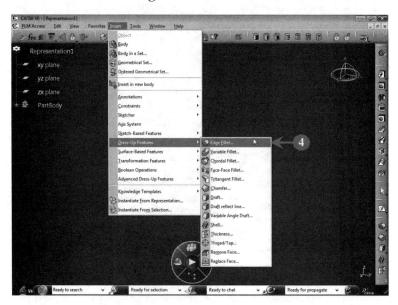

FIGURE 3.43

The **Edge Fillet Definition** dialog box appears with the default setting of Radius with no edge selected, as shown in **Figure 3.44**:

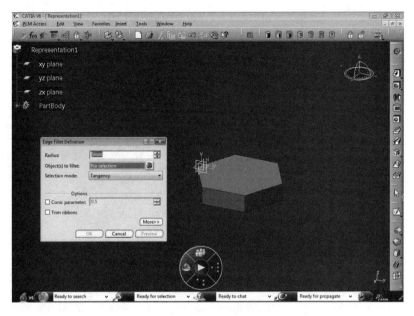

FIGURE 3.44

5. *Select* the edges that you want to fillet. The number of selected edges would be shown in the **Object(s) to fillet** box in the **Edge Fillet Definition** dialog box (**Figure 3.45**).

6. *Click* the **OK** button in the **Edge Fillet Definition** dialog box, as shown in Figure 3.45:

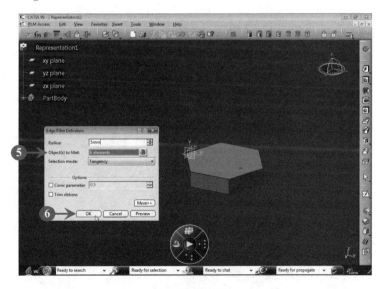

FIGURE 3.45

The final, edge-filleted solid model is shown in **Figure 3.46**:

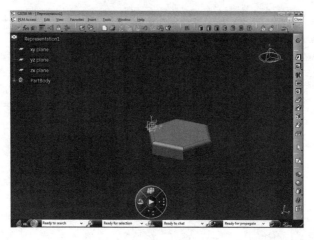

FIGURE 3.46

Figure 3.46 shows the final solid hexagon after filleting all the edges. We next discuss the addition of a variable radius fillet to a solid model.

The Variable Radius Fillet Feature

The variable radius fillet feature is used to apply fillets of varied radius to the different edges of the solid models.

Perform the following steps to create a variable radius filleted solid model:

1. *Create* a solid model from the sketch of a parallelogram by using the pad feature, as shown in **Figure 3.47**:

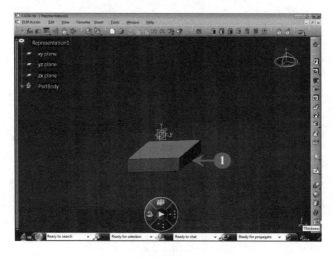

FIGURE 3.47

2. *Select* the **Insert > Dress-Up Features > Variable Fillet** to use the variable radius fillet feature, as shown in **Figure 3.48**:

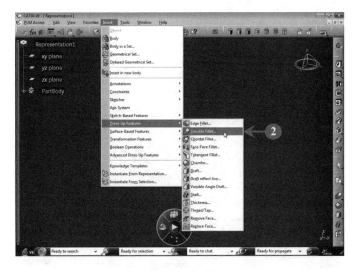

FIGURE 3.48

The **Variable Radius Fillet Definition** dialog box appears with the default values of radius and none of the edges selected, as shown in **Figure 3.49:**

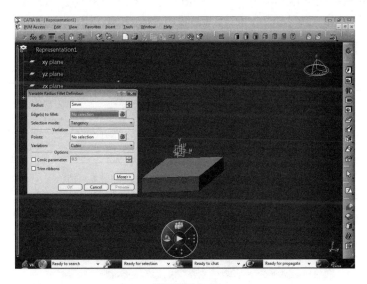

FIGURE 3.49

3. *Select* the edge you want to fillet. The number of selected edges is shown in the **Edge(s) to fillet** box (**Figure 3.50**).

4. *Set* the radius of the fillet by entering the appropriate value in the **Radius** option. In our case, we set the radius of the fillet applied on Edge2 to 5 mm, as shown in Figure 3.50:

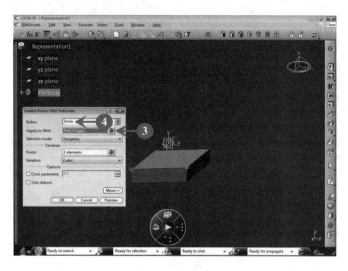

FIGURE 3.50

5. *Repeat* steps 3 and 4 to set the radius of the other edges. In our case, we have entered the radius of the second edge as 15 mm (**Figure 3.51**).

6. *Click* the **OK** button in the **Variable Radius Fillet Definition** dialog box, as shown in Figure 3.51:

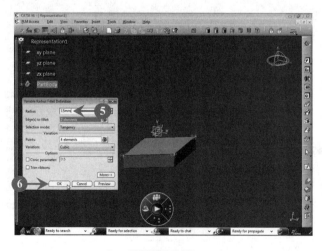

FIGURE 3.51

The preview of the solid model is shown in **Figure 3.52**:

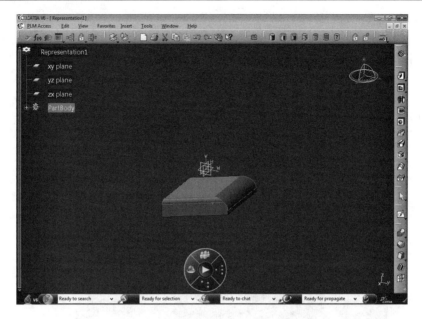

FIGURE 3.52

Figure 3.52 shows the preview after the variable radius fillet of radii 5 mm and 15 mm are added to the solid model.

The final solid model is shown in **Figure 3.53**:

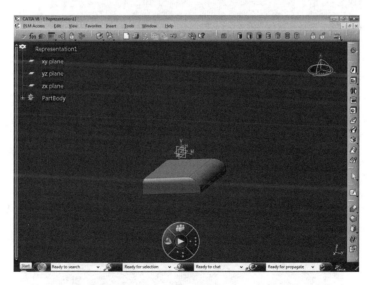

FIGURE 3.53

After discussing the variable radius fillet feature, we next discuss the face–face fillet feature of the fillet group.

The Face–Face Fillet Feature

The face–face fillet feature is applied on the adjacent edges of a solid model. To apply the face–face fillet, first the faces of the solid model are selected and then the face–face fillet feature is applied.

Perform the following steps to create a face–face filleted solid model:

1. *Create* a sketch consisting of two concentric circles in the Sketcher workbench (**Figure 3.54**).

2. *Select* the **Exit workbench** button (⬚) from the Sketcher workbench, as shown in Figure 3.54:

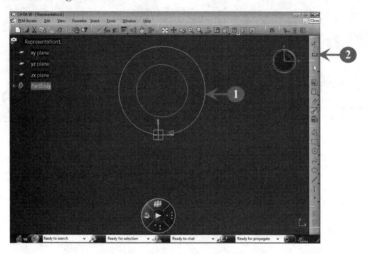

FIGURE 3.54

The sketch drawn is displayed in the Part Design workbench, as shown in **Figure 3.55**:

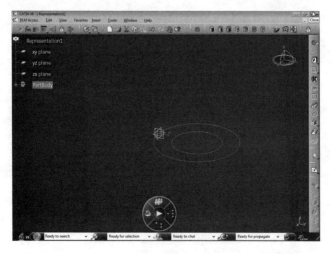

FIGURE 3.55

3. *Create* a solid model by using the pad feature in the Part Design workbench, as shown in **Figure 3.56**:

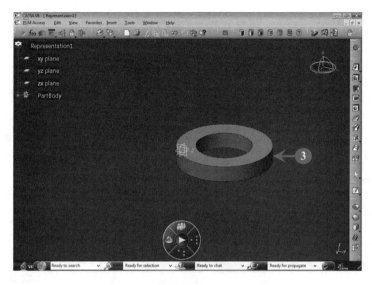

FIGURE 3.56

4. *Select* **Insert > Dress-Up Features > Face–Face Fillet** to select the face–face fillet feature, as shown in **Figure 3.57**:

FIGURE 3.57

The **Face–Face Fillet Definition** dialog box appears with default values, as shown in **Figure 3.58**:

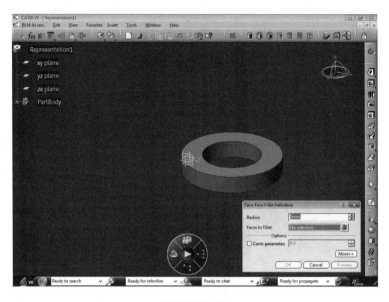

FIGURE 3.58

5. *Select* the faces that you want to fillet. In our case, the outer and inner faces are selected on which the face–face fillet feature would be applied. The number of selected faces is shown in the **Faces to fillet** box of the **Face–Face Fillet Definition** dialog box (**Figure 3.59**).

6. *Click* the **OK** button, as shown in **Figure 3.59**:

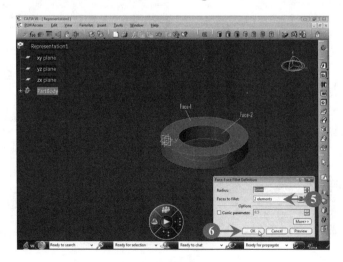

FIGURE 3.59

The final solid model is shown in **Figure 3.60**:

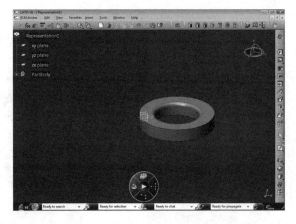

FIGURE 3.60

After discussing the face–face fillet feature, we next learn how to apply the tritangent fillet feature to solid models.

The Tritangent Fillet Feature

You apply the tritangent feature by first selecting the two supporting faces and then selecting the face that would be removed to create the desired solid model. The filleted part of the sketch is tangent to the selected surfaces.

Perform the following steps to add a tritangent fillet feature to the selected part of a solid:

1. *Create* a solid model of the sketch by using the pad feature in the Part Design workbench. In our case, the solid model created by using the pad feature is from the design of a parallelogram, as shown in **Figure 3.61**:

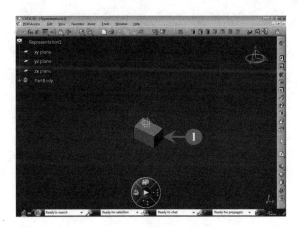

FIGURE 3.61

2. *Select* **Insert > Dress-Up Features > Tritangent Fillet**, as shown in **Figure 3.62**:

FIGURE 3.62

The tritangent fillet feature is selected and the **Tritangent Fillet Definition** dialog box opens (**Figure 3.63**).

3. *Select* the first face of the solid model to fillet, as shown in Figure 3.63:

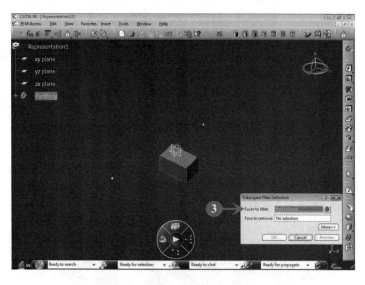

FIGURE 3.63

4. *Enable* the rotating of the solid model by using the **View>Rotate** option, as shown in **Figure 3.64**:

FIGURE 3.64

The solid model is rotated by *selecting* the **face 1 face in clockwise direction**. After rotation the opposite face of the solid model is visible, as shown in **Figure 3.65**:

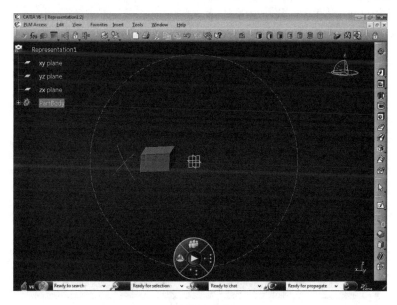

FIGURE 3.65

5. *Select* the second face (opposite to the previously selected face) to fillet, as shown in **Figure 3.66**:

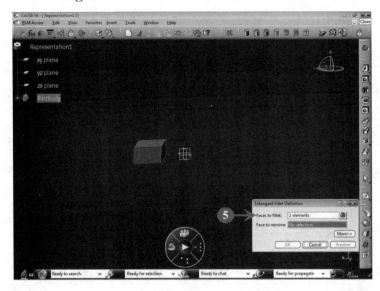

FIGURE 3.66

6. *Select* that face of the solid model that will be filleted (**Figure 3.67**). In our case, Pad.1\Face.3 is selected.

7. *Click* the **OK** button in the **Tritangent Fillet Definition** dialog box, as shown in Figure 3.67:

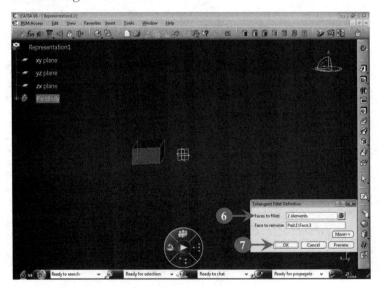

FIGURE 3.67

The final tritangent filleted solid model is shown in **Figure 3.68**:

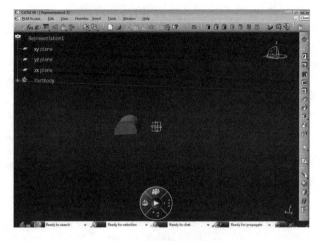

FIGURE 3.68

After discussing the tritangent fillet feature, we next learn how to chamfer the sketches by using the chamfer feature.

The Chamfer Feature

The chamfer feature is used to add a bevel face to the edge of a solid model. The chamfer feature is applied to any edge of a solid model. However, in the case of chamfering adjacent faces of a solid model, the angle of the surface should always be less than 90 degrees.

Perform the following steps to create a chamfered solid model:

1. *Create* a solid model from a parallelogram sketched in the Sketcher workbench, as shown in **Figure 3.69**:

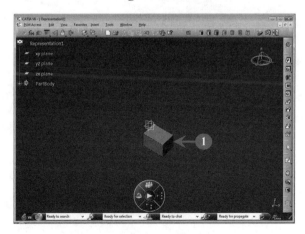

FIGURE 3.69

2. *Select* **Insert>Dress-Up Features>Chamfer**, as shown in **Figure 3.70**:

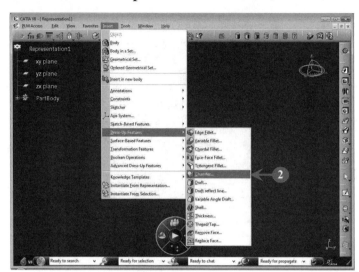

FIGURE 3.70

The chamfer feature is selected and the **Chamfer Definition** dialog box appears with the default values, as shown in **Figure 3.71**:

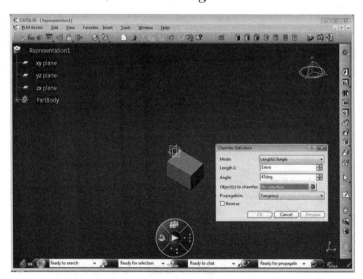

FIGURE 3.71

3. *Select* any edge of the solid model to chamfer (**Figure 3.72**).
4. *Click* the **OK** button in the **Chamfer Definition** dialog box, as shown in Figure 3.72:

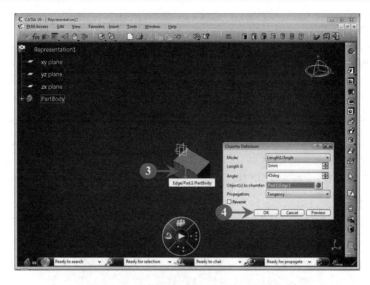

FIGURE 3.72

Note: If any face of a solid model is selected to chamfer, then all the edges would be chamfered.

The final chamfered sketch is shown in **Figure 3.73**:

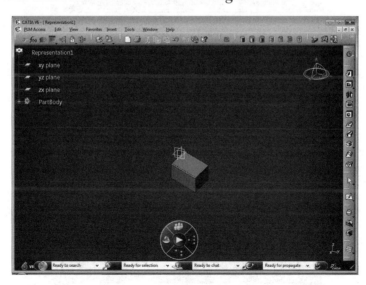

FIGURE 3.73

After discussing the chamfer feature, we next learn how to use the draft feature on a solid model.

The Draft Feature

The draft feature is used to create a model by casting or molding a part of a solid model. The process of drafting is done by tapering the solid model along its edges while preserving the basic structure of the model. The value of the taper angle specifies the extent of the drafting of the solid model. The taper angle is an angle by which the supporting edges are bent. However, the taper angle should be less than 90 degrees.

Perform the following steps to create a drafted solid model:

1. *Create* the model of a solid that you want to draft. In our case, a solid model of a parallelogram sketched in the Sketcher workbench is created, as shown in **Figure 3.74**:

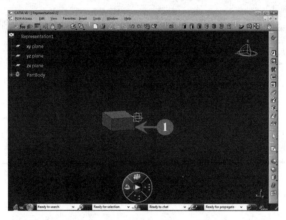

FIGURE 3.74

2. *Select* **Insert > Dress-Up Features > Draft**, as shown in **Figure 3.75**:

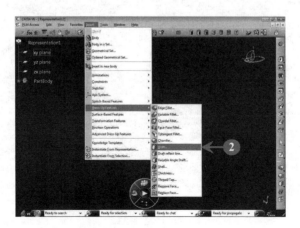

FIGURE 3.75

The draft feature is selected and the **Draft Definition** dialog box appears (**Figure 3.76**). It contains the default values for the faces to be drafted and the angle for drafting of the faces as 5 degrees, and the selection of a neutral element, as shown in **Figure 3.76**:

FIGURE 3.76

3. *Enter* the desired angle by which you want the draft to be created. In our case, we have entered **50deg** (degree) (**Figure 3.77**).

4. *Select* the face of the solid that would be drafted (Figure 3.77). The **Face(s) to draft** box in the **Draft Definition** dialog box changes according to the selected faces. In our case, the number of faces to draft is **2**.

5. *Select* the neutral element. In our case, we have selected **Pad.1\Face.3** (Figure 3.77).

6. *Click* the **OK** button in the **Draft Definition** dialog box, as shown in Figure 3.77:

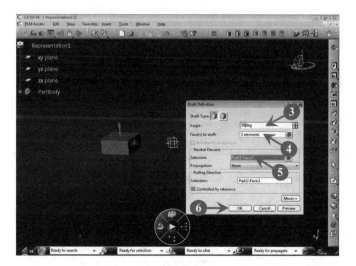

FIGURE 3.77

The final drafted sketch is shown in **Figure 3.78**:

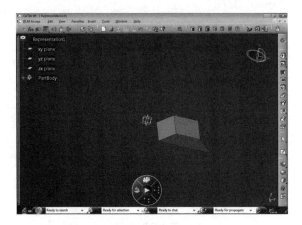

FIGURE 3.78

Figure 3.78 shows the figure after drafting a solid model by a taper angle of 50 degrees. After discussing the draft, we next discuss how to use a shell feature on a solid model.

The Shell Feature

The shell feature is used to create a solid model by removing the selected parts of a solid model in such a manner that the thickness of the sides remain. In other words, the shell feature removes the selected part of the entire solid model by a specified thickness.

Perform the following steps to create a shelled solid model:

1. *Create* a solid model that you want to shell. In our case, the solid model is created from a sketch of a parallelogram, as shown in **Figure 3.79**:

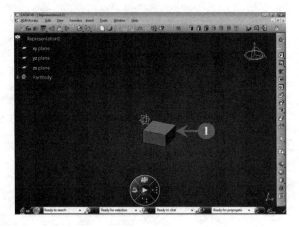

FIGURE 3.79

2. *Select* **Insert > Dress-Up Features > Shell**, as shown in **Figure 3.80**:

FIGURE 3.80

The shell feature is selected and the **Shell Definition** dialog box appears (**Figure 3.81**).

3. *Select* the face of the solid that would be removed to create a shelled solid model (Figure 3.81). **The Faces to remove** box in the **Shell Definition** dialog box changes according to the selected faces. In our case, **Pad.1\Face.1** is selected (Figure 3.81).

4. *Click* the **OK** button, as shown in Figure 3.81:

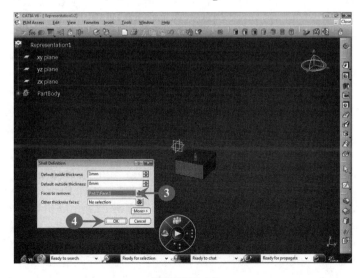

FIGURE 3.81

The final shelled model is displayed in **Figure 3.82**:

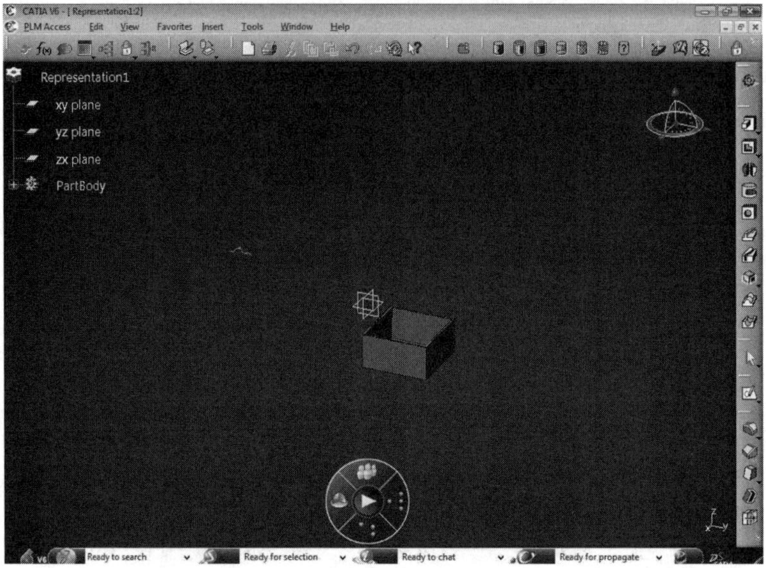

FIGURE 3.82

After discussing the shell feature, the entire section on the dress-up features of the Part Design workbench is complete.

The application of the dress-up features, such as fillet, chamfer, draft, and shell, to solid models has been discussed. For example, you have learned to apply different types of fillet features to the solid models. Then the chamfer feature was used to chamfer a solid model. Next, the drafted solid model was created by using the draft feature. In the end, the shell feature was used to create a thin structure.

In the next section, we discuss the transformation features that are applied to the solid models.

3.3 USING TRANSFORMATION FEATURES

Apart from the sketch-based and dress-up features that are applied on solid models, the transformation features are used to transform the solid models along a reference. For example, the solid model can be moved, rotated, mirrored, scaled, and patterned by using the transformation features. Moreover, the basic structure of the solid model is not altered by applying the transformation features. For example, if the rotation is used to create a solid model, then the base of the solid model is not altered by rotation; only the orientation changes. Following are the noteworthy transformation features that are used to transform the solid models:

- The translation feature
- The rotation feature
- The symmetry feature
- The mirror feature
- The pattern feature

First, we discuss the translation feature.

The Translation Feature

The translation feature is applied on a solid model to displace it in a specific direction by selecting a plane and a specified distance in the Part Design workbench. The translation feature is used in designing solid models.

Perform the following steps to create a translated solid model:

1. *Create* a sketch in the Sketcher workbench. In our case, we have created a hexagon (**Figure 3.83**).
2. *Select* the **Exit workbench** button (⬚) from the Sketcher workbench, as shown in Figure 3.83:

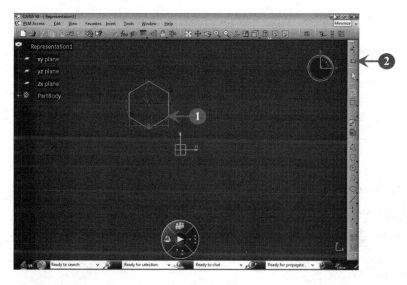

FIGURE 3.83

The sketch is displayed in the Part Design workbench, as shown in **Figure 3.84**:

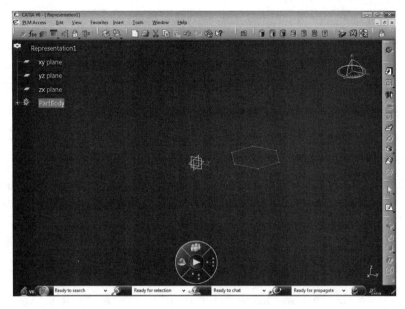

FIGURE 3.84

3. *Create* a solid model using the pad feature (**Figure 3.85**).

4. *Select* **Insert > Transformation Features > Translation**, as shown in Figure 3.85:

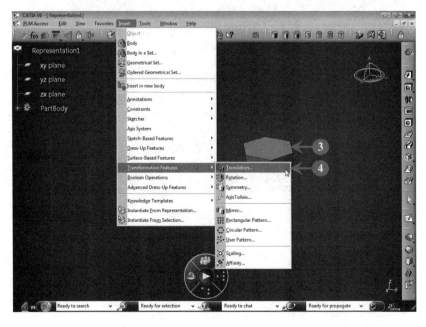

FIGURE 3.85

The **Question** message box appears and prompts the user to either keep the transformation specifications or not (**Figure 3.86**).

5. *Click* the **Yes** button in the **Question** message box, as shown in Figure 3.86:

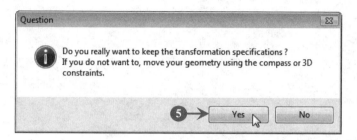

FIGURE 3.86

The **Translate Definition** dialog box is activated in which the **Direction, distance** option is selected by default in the **Vector Definition** drop-down list and the focus is on the **Distance** box.

> **Note:** The other options are **Point to Point** and **Coordinates** that may be selected to specify the direction of the translation. In the case of **Point to Point** translation, you need to specify the starting and end point along which the solid model would be translated. In addition, to translate using the **Coordinates** option, you need to specify all of the coordinates.

6. *Select* the direction in the **Direction** option for the plane representations, along which the solid will be translated. In our case, we *select* the **xy-plane** (**Figure 3.87**).

> **Note:** You can also *right-click* on the **Distance** option and *select* a particular plane in which the translation would be directed.

7. *Enter* the distance by which the solid model would be translated. In our case, we set the distance as 50 mm (Figure 3.87).
8. *Click* the **OK** button in the **Translate Definition** dialog box, as shown in Figure 3.87:

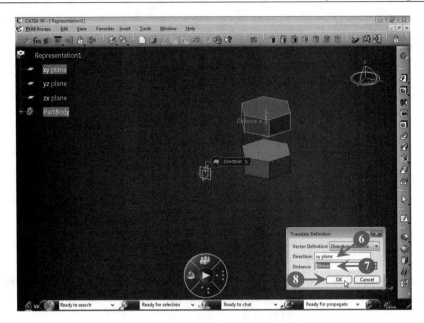

FIGURE 3.87

The final translated solid model is shown in **Figure 3.88**:

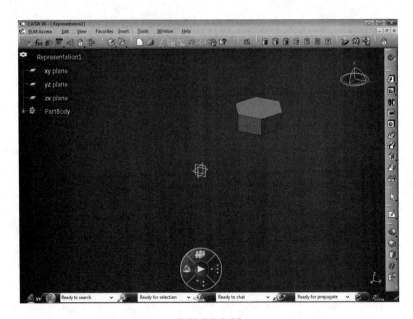

FIGURE 3.88

In Figure 3.88, the solid model is translated by 50 mm from the initial position in the direction of the *xy*-plane. This ends the section on translation of a solid model. After discussing the translation of a solid model, we next discuss how to rotate a solid model.

The Rotation Feature

The rotation feature is applied to a solid model to rotate the solid model about an axis. The utility of the rotation feature is to analyze the changes on the structure, symmetry, and orientation of the solid model after rotating the solid model. Depending upon the results of the rotation, the modifications in the model can be further improved.

Perform the following steps to rotate a solid model:

1. *Create* a solid model in the Part Design workbench that you want to rotate. In our case, the solid model is a parallelogram created in the Sketcher workbench, as shown in **Figure 3.89**:

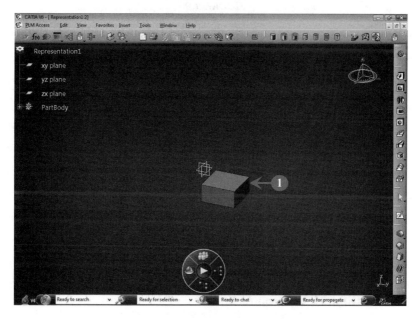

FIGURE 3.89

2. *Select* **Insert > Transformation Features > Rotation**, as shown in **Figure 3.90**:

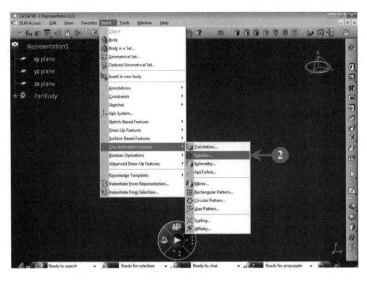

FIGURE 3.90

The **Question** message box appears and prompts the user to either keep the transformation specification or not (**Figure 3.91**).

3. *Click* the **Yes** button, as shown in Figure 3.91:

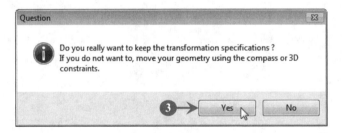

FIGURE 3.91

The **Rotate Definition** dialog box is activated with a focus on the **Angle** and the cursor on the **Axis** options (**Figure 3.92**). The **Axis–Angle** option is selected in the **Definition Mode** drop-down list.

> **Note:** Other options are **Axis-Two Elements** and **Three Points**, which may be selected to specify the axis and angle of the rotation.

In the **Axis** box, select the axis of rotation. In the **Angle** box, select the angle of rotation.

4. *Select* one of the edges of the solid model as the axis of the rotation of the solid model, as shown in Figure 3.92:

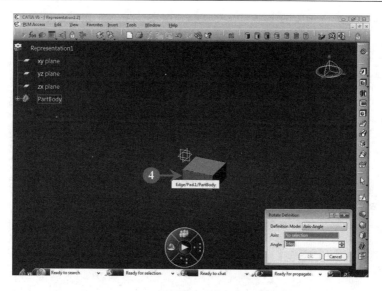

FIGURE 3.92

5. *Enter* the angle of rotation as 90 deg (**Figure 3.93**). The preview of the rotated solid model is displayed in Figure 3.93.

6. *Click* the **OK** button, as shown in Figure 3.93:

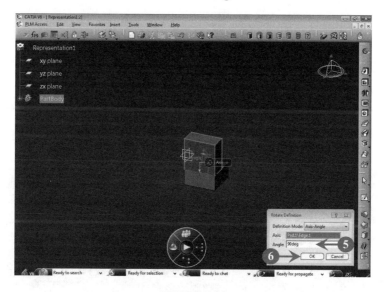

FIGURE 3.93

The final rotated solid model after rotation to the desired angle and axis is shown in **Figure 3.94**:

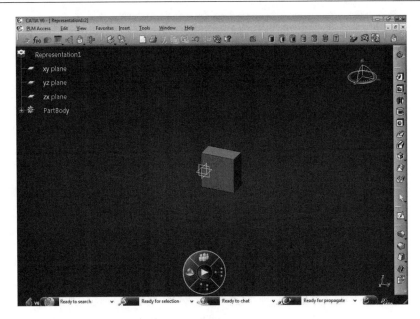

FIGURE 3.94

After discussing the rotation of the figure, we next learn how to add the symmetry feature to a solid model.

The Symmetry Feature

The symmetry feature refers to the similar pattern or shape of a sketch or design with respect to a reference, such as the axis of symmetry. In other words, the images on both sides of the axis of symmetry must be the same in the case of a symmetric axis. The axis of symmetry lies in the middle. In contrast, the images on both sides of an axis of symmetry need not be the same. Symmetric as well asymmetric shapes are shown in **Figure 3.95**:

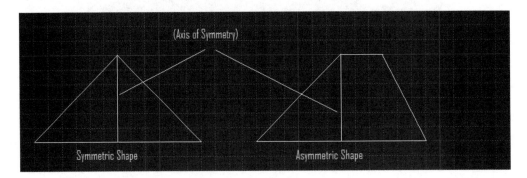

FIGURE 3.95

Figure 3.95 shows two figures:

- **Symmetric figure:** Both sides of the axis of symmetry are equal in shape and orientation
- **Asymmetric figure:** Both sides of the axis of symmetry are not similar

In CATIA V6, the symmetric solid model is created by flipping a solid model around a point, line, plane, or a face. These are called reference elements. The utility of the symmetry feature is to create a symmetrical solid model where the shape and orientation is similar with respect to a reference element.

Perform the following steps to create a symmetric solid model:

1. *Create* a solid model in Part Design workbench. In our case, the solid model is a circle created in the Sketcher workbench, as shown in **Figure 3.96**:

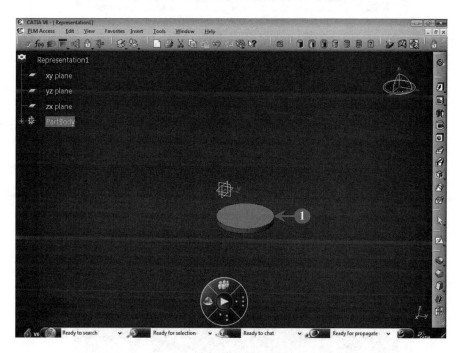

FIGURE 3.96

2. *Select* **Insert > Transformation Features > Symmetry**, as shown in **Figure 3.97**:

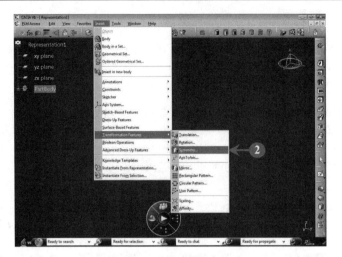

FIGURE 3.97

The **Question** dialog box appears.

3. *Click* the **Yes** button. The **Symmetry Definition** dialog box is activated with a focus on the **Reference** box (**Figure 3.98**).
4. *Select* the face of the solid model along which the reference element is created (Figure 3.98).
5. *Click* the **OK** button in the **Symmetry Definition** dialog box, as shown in Figure 3.98:

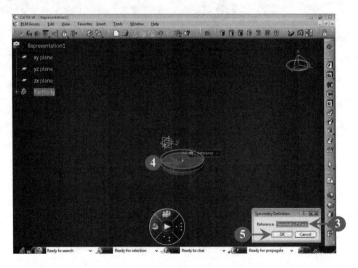

FIGURE 3.98

The final symmetric figure of the solid model is shown in **Figure 3.99**:

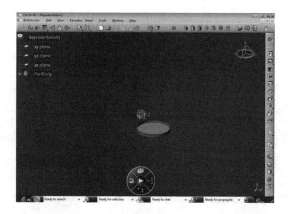

FIGURE 3.99

In Figure 3.99, a symmetric solid model is created by flipping the solid model by the selected face.

After creating the symmetry of a solid model, we next learn to mirror solid models.

The Mirror Feature

The mirror feature is used to mirror either a part of or the entire solid model. The initial sketch can be mirrored either along a plane or a face. When the mirror feature is added to a solid model, the initial part is retained and the mirror of the solid model is created.

Perform the following steps to create a mirrored solid model:

1. *Select* the face of a solid model created. In our case, we have selected the face of a semicircle, as shown in **Figure 3.100**:

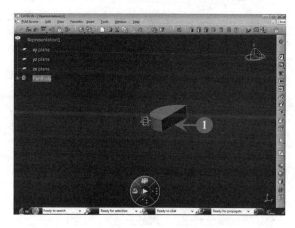

FIGURE 3.100

2. *Select* **Insert** > **Transformation Features** > **Mirror**, as shown in **Figure 3.101**:

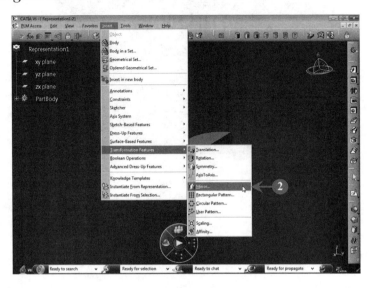

FIGURE 3.101

The **Mirror Definition** dialog box appears with the selected edge and a preview of the mirrored image (**Figure 3.102**).

3. *Click* the **OK** button, as shown in Figure 3.102:

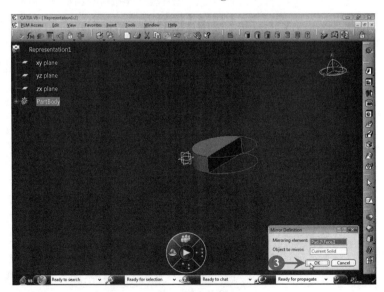

FIGURE 3.102

The final mirrored solid model is shown in **Figure 3.103**:

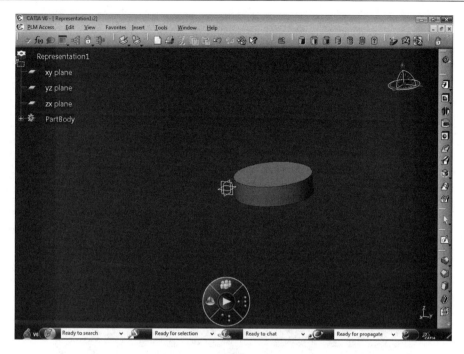

FIGURE 3.103

Figure 3.103 shows the mirrored solid model. After discussing the mirroring of a solid model, we next learn how to create patterned solid models using the pattern feature.

The Pattern Feature

A pattern refers to a specific design. In CATIA V6, a patterned solid model is a solid model that has a continuous pattern designed throughout its entire face. CATIA V6 provides the following types of pattern features to create a patterned solid model:

- The rectangular pattern feature
- The circular pattern feature

We next discuss how to use the rectangular pattern feature to create a rectangular-patterned solid model.

The Rectangular Pattern Feature

The rectangular pattern feature is used to arrange the selected item in a rectangular manner. In other words, by using the rectangular pattern feature, you can arrange any shape, such as a rectangle, circle, or hexagon, to the solid model in a rectangular way. CATIA V6 provides a **Rectangular Pattern** button (▦) on the **Pattern** sub-toolbar to add a rectangular pattern to a solid model.

Perform the following steps to add the rectangular pattern to a solid model:

1. *Create* a solid model of a parallelogram in the Part Design workbench on which the rectangular pattern will be added, as shown in **Figure 3.104**:

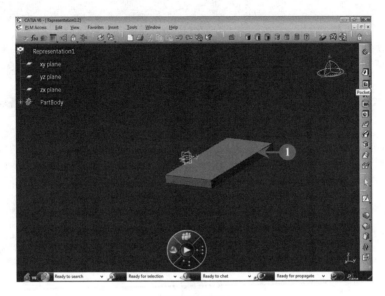

FIGURE 3.104

2. *Open* the sketch in the Sketcher workbench in the *xy*-plane, as shown in **Figure 3.105**:

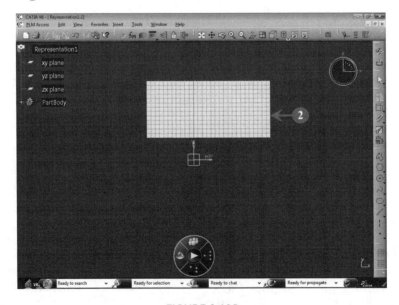

FIGURE 3.105

3. *Add* the shape to the sketch. In our case, a hexagon is added to the solid model, as shown in **Figure 3.106**:

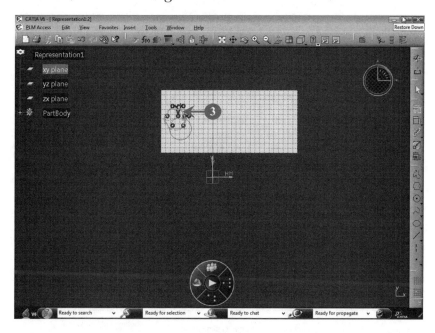

FIGURE 3.106

4. *Open* the sketch in the Part Design workbench, as shown in **Figure 3.107**:

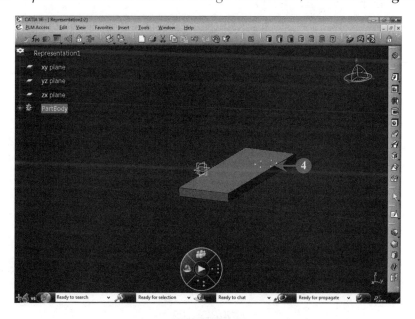

FIGURE 3.107

5. *Add* a pocket to the solid model. The solid model after adding the pocket is shown in **Figure 3.108**:

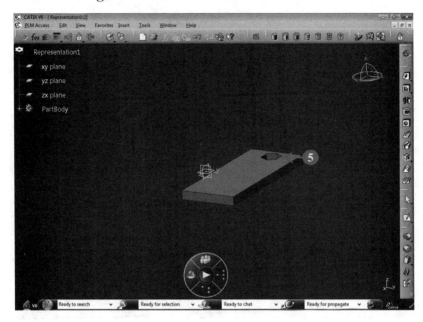

FIGURE 3.108

6. *Select* **Insert > Transformation Features > Rectangular Pattern**, as shown in **Figure 3.109**:

FIGURE 3.109

The **Rectangular Pattern Definition** dialog box appears (**Figure 3.110**).

The **Rectangular Pattern Definition** dialog box contains the following options required to add a pattern:

- **Parameters:** Selects a parameter for pattern, such as length and space
- **Instance(s):** Specifies the number of instances of the pattern created
- **Spacing:** Specifies the space between two instances of shapes
- **Reference element:** Specifies the face, line, or axis of the solid along which the pattern should be added
- **Object:** Selects the object on the solid model that is to be patterned

7. *Select* the option from the **Parameters** drop-down list. In our case, we select **Instance(s)** & **Spacing** (Figure 3.110).

8. *Select* the number of instances of the pattern as **4** in the **Instance(s)** box (Figure 3.110).

9. *Select* the spacing between instances as 30 mm in the **Spacing** box (Figure 3.110).

10. *Select* the face of the solid along which the pattern should be added by specifying the Reference element (Figure 3.110). The Reference element in the **Rectangular Pattern Definition** dialog box shows the selected face of the solid model. In our case, the Reference element is **Pad.5\Face.7**.

11. *Select* the pocket, which is added as a pattern in the solid model. In our case, it is a hexagon (Figure 3.110).

12. *Click* the **OK** button, as shown in Figure 3.110:

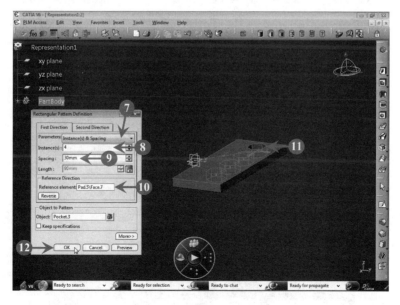

FIGURE 3.110

The final rectangular-patterned solid model is displayed in **Figure 3.111**:

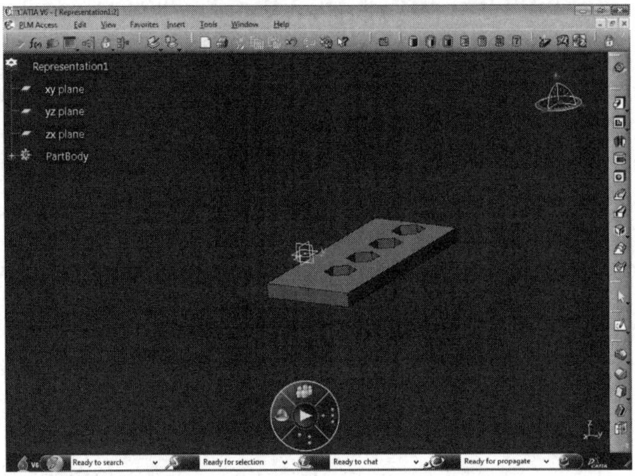

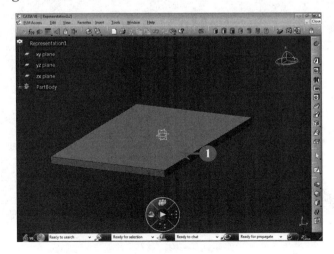

FIGURE 3.111

After discussing the rectangular pattern, we next learn how to add a circular pattern to a solid model.

The Circular Pattern Feature

The circular pattern feature is used to arrange a selected item in a circular manner. In other words, you can arrange any shape, such as rectangle, hexagon, spline, or circle, on a solid model in a circular manner.

Perform the following steps to add a circular pattern feature to a solid model.

1. *Create* a solid model in the Part Design workbench to which the pattern will be added. In our case the solid model created is a rectangle, as shown in **Figure 3.112**:

FIGURE 3.112

2. *Open* the solid model in the *xy*-plane of the Sketcher workbench to add a circular pattern, as shown in **Figure 3.113**:

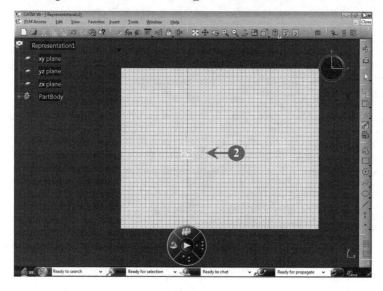

FIGURE 3.113

3. *Add* the shape to the sketch in the Sketcher workbench. In our case we add a circle, as shown in **Figure 3.114**:

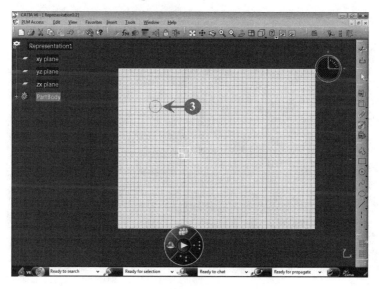

FIGURE 3.114

4. *Open* the sketch in the Part Design workbench, as shown in **Figure 3.115**:

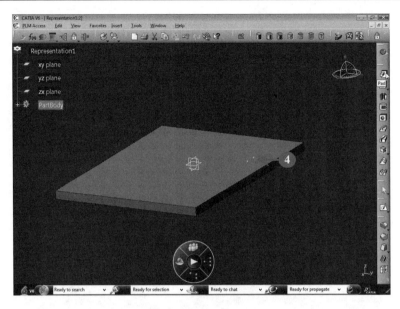

FIGURE 3.115

5. *Add* a pocket to the solid model. The figure of the solid model after adding the pocket is shown in **Figure 3.116**:

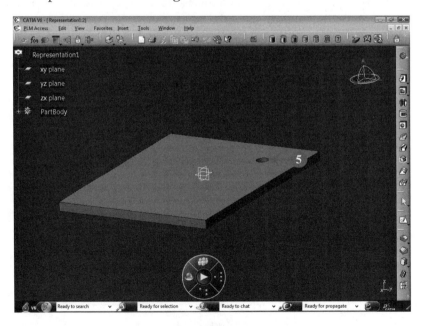

FIGURE 3.116

6. *Select* **Insert>Transformation Features>Circular Pattern**, as shown in **Figure 3.117**:

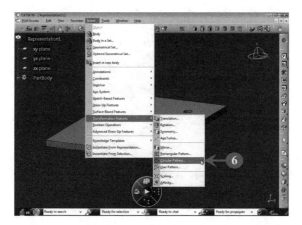

FIGURE 3.117

The **Circular Pattern Definition** dialog box appears (**Figure 3.118**).

7. *Enter* the instances of the patterns as **12** in the **Instance(s)** box (Figure 3.118).
8. *Enter* the angular spacing between the instances as **45 deg** in the **Angular spacing** box (Figure 3.118).
9. *Select* the reference element on which the pattern will be added (Figure 3.118). The Reference element in the **Circular Pattern Definition** dialog box shows the selected face of the solid model. In our case, the Reference element is **Pad.6\Face.8** (Figure 3.118).
10. *Select* the pocket that is added as a pattern (Figure 3.118). The preview is displayed (Figure 3.118).
11. *Click* the **OK** button, as shown in Figure 3.118:

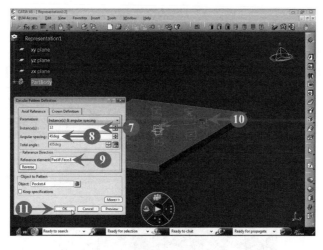

FIGURE 3.118

The final circular-patterned solid model is shown in **Figure 3.119**:

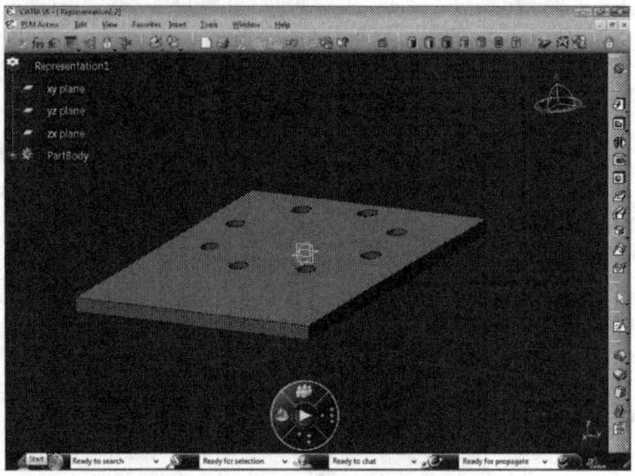

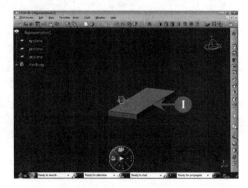

FIGURE 3.119

Now, with the creation of the circular pattern, the discussion on transformation features is complete.

In this section, you have learned to transform solid models using transformation features such as translation, rotation, symmetry, mirroring, and patterns (rectangular and circular). We next learn how to insert additional bodies into a solid model.

3.4 INSERTING ADDITIONAL BODIES INTO SOLID MODELS

Apart from creating different solid models by adding features to the solid models in the Part Design workbench, you can also insert additional bodies into the existing solid models. The additional bodies are included under the **PartBody** node of the specification tree. When an additional body is added, the new body, Body.2, is added to the specification tree.

Perform the following steps to insert an additional body into an existing solid model:

1. *Create* the solid model to which you want to insert a body. In our case, a solid model of a rectangle is created, as shown in **Figure 3.120**:

FIGURE 3.120

2. *Select* **Insert**>**Body** to add another body into the already existing model, as shown in **Figure 3.121**.

FIGURE 3.121

The new body (Body.2) is added in the specification tree, as shown in **Figure 3.122**:

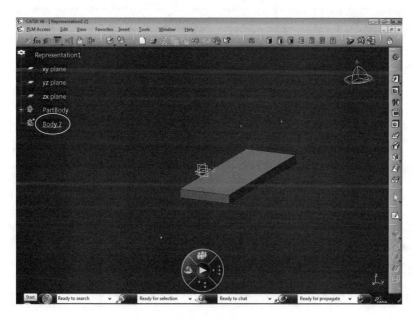

FIGURE 3.122

In the specification tree, the addition of **Body.2** allows you to add any new sketch to the initial sketch.

3. *Open* the sketch in the Sketcher workbench in *xy*-plane, as shown in **Figure 3.123**:

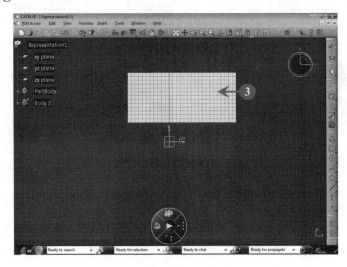

FIGURE 3.123

4. *Add* the new sketch to the existing solid model, as shown in **Figure 3.124**:

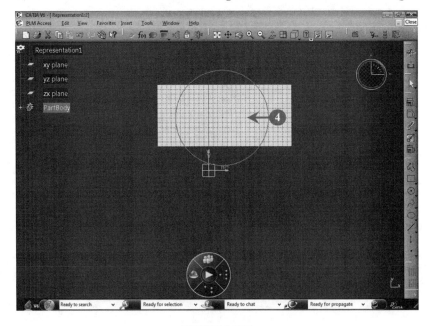

FIGURE 3.124

5. *Open* the sketch in the Part Design workbench. The new sketch is added as the additional body (Body.2) and is also shown in the specification tree, as shown in **Figure 3.125**:

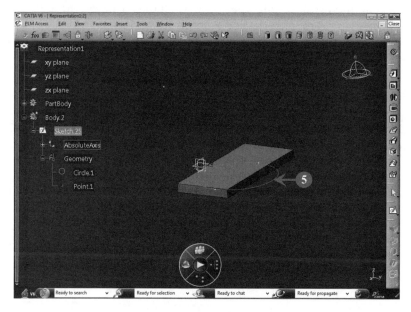

FIGURE 3.125

6. *Create* the final solid model using the pad feature. The final sketch with the additional solid body added is shown in **Figure 3.126**:

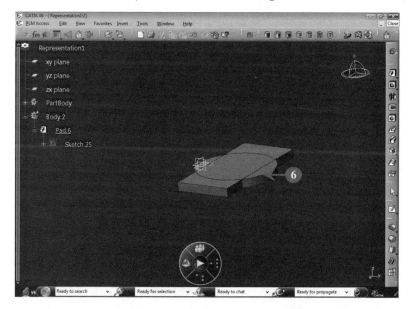

FIGURE 3.126

After inserting the additional body to a solid model, this section is complete. You have learned about the Part Design workbench in detail, including the sketch-based, dress-up, and transformation features. In addition, you also learned to create and modify different types of solid models using all three features. Lastly, you have learned to add additional bodies to a solid model.

With this, we have reached the end of this chapter. Let's summarize what you learned in this chapter.

SUMMARY

In this chapter, you learned about:

- The Part Design workbench
- Sketch-based features, such as pad, shaft, and rib
- Dress-up features, such as fillet, and chamfer
- Transformation features, such as translations, mirrors, and patterns
- Adding an additional body to the existing solid models

Chapter 4

ASSEMBLY DESIGN WORKBENCH

In This Chapter

◊ Creating an Assembly
◊ Working with Assembly Components
◊ Using Assembly Features
◊ Summary

In the last chapter, you learned how to create individual solid models using the Part Design workbench of CATIA V6. The current chapter takes you one step forward in the same direction by describing how to create designs that consist of two or more solid models. Such designs are known as assemblies and can be created in the Assembly Design workbench of CATIA V6. The process of creating assemblies is known as assembly modeling.

This chapter begins with a discussion on how to create an assembly. Then you learn how to work with assembly components, such as replacing, showing, and hiding an assembly component. Finally, the various assembly features are discussed.

We first begin with creating an assembly.

4.1 CREATING AN ASSEMBLY

We first create the individual components for the assembly in the Part Design workbench and then combine those components to form the assembly in the Assembly Design workbench. Therefore, the task of creating an assembly is divided into the following two subtasks:

1. Creating components for the assembly
2. Assembling the components

We next learn to perform these subtasks.

Creating Components for the Assembly

You can create components for an assembly in the Part Design workbench of CATIA V6. To create a component, you first need to draw the sketch of the component. The Sketcher workbench can be used to draw the sketch of the component. After that, you can convert this sketch into a solid model in the Part Design workbench.

Perform the following steps to create components for an assembly:

1. *Open* CATIA V6.
2. *Select* **Start > Mechanical Design > Part Design** on the CATIA V6 user interface to start the Part Design workbench, as shown in **Figure 4.1**:

FIGURE 4.1

The **3D Shape/Representation DS** dialog box opens (**Figure 4.2**).

3. *Enter* a name for the first component in the **Representation Name** text box (Figure 4.2). In our case, we have entered **Part1**.
4. *Click* the **Finish** button to close the **3D Shape/Representation DS** dialog box, as shown in Figure 4.2:

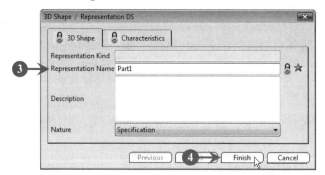

FIGURE 4.2

The first component, **Part1**, is created in the Part Design workbench (**Figure 4.3**). Now, you need to draw the sketch of the component using the Sketcher workbench. You can invoke the Sketcher workbench by first *clicking* the **Sketch** button on the **Sketcher** toolbar and then *selecting* a sketching plane from the specification tree.

5.   *Click* the **Sketch** button on the **Sketcher** toolbar (Figure 4.3).

6.   *Select* the ***xy-plane*** option in the specification tree, as shown in Figure 4.3:

FIGURE 4.3

The Sketcher workbench is displayed with the *xy*-plane as the sketching plane (**Figure 4.4**).

7.   *Draw* a sketch in the Sketcher workbench (Figure 4.4).

8.   *Click* the **Exit workbench** button on the Workbench toolbar to exit the Sketcher workbench, as shown in Figure 4.4:

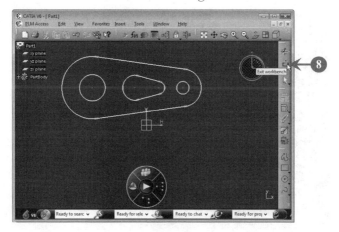

FIGURE 4.4

The Sketcher workbench closes and the Part Design workbench gets displayed, as shown in **Figure 4.5**:

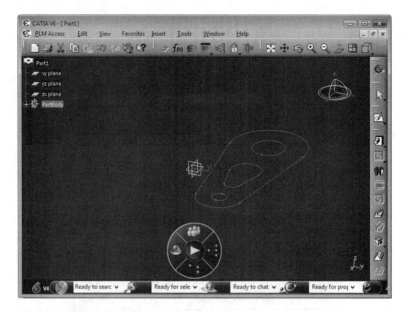

FIGURE 4.5

After you have drawn the sketch of the assembly component, you need to convert the sketch into a solid model. You can convert a sketch into a solid model by using the pad feature available in the Part Design workbench.

9.   *Select* **Insert > Sketch-Based Features > Pad** from the menu bar to apply the pad feature to the sketch that you have drawn in the Sketcher workbench, as shown in **Figure 4.6**:

FIGURE 4.6

The **Pad Definition** dialog box opens and the preview of the solid model generated from the sketch gets displayed (**Figure 4.7**).

10. *Click* the **OK** button in the **Pad Definition** dialog box, as shown in **Figure 4.7**:

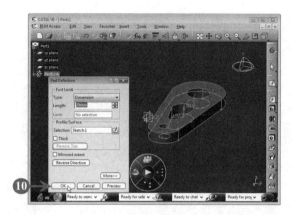

FIGURE 4.7

The **Pad Definition** dialog box closes and the first component for the assembly is created. Now, you need to create other assembly components. In our case, we create three more assembly components, which have the same basic geometries as that of the three empty portions of the first assembly component.

11. *Repeat* steps 2 to 10 to create the second component for the assembly that can fit into the first empty portion of the **Part1** component, as shown in **Figure 4.8**:

FIGURE 4.8

12. *Repeat* steps 2 to 10 to create the third component for the assembly that can fit into the second empty portion of the **Part1** component, as shown in **Figure 4.9**:

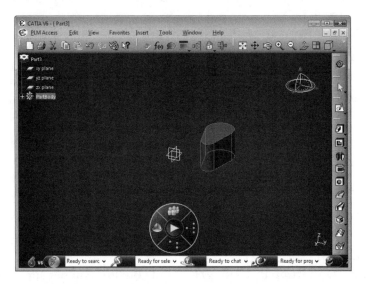

FIGURE 4.9

13. *Repeat* steps 2 to 10 to create the fourth component for your assembly that can fit into the third empty portion of the **Part1** component, as shown in **Figure 4.10**:

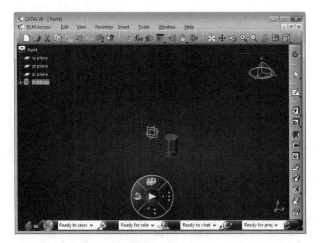

FIGURE 4.10

Once you have created all the required components for your assembly, you can combine those components to form the assembly. The next section discusses how to assemble individual assembly components.

Assembling the Components

Start the Assembly Design workbench to create an assembly from individual assembly components. When you start the Assembly Design workbench, by default a blank assembly is created. You can then add all the components to the blank assembly to form the final assembly.

Perform the following steps to learn how to assemble different components to create an assembly:

1. *Select* **Start>Mechanical Design>Assembly Design** on the CATIA V6 user interface to start the Assembly Design workbench, as shown in **Figure 4.11**:

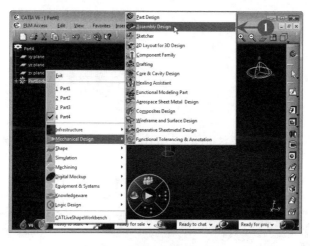

FIGURE 4.11

The **Start – Step 1 – Product** dialog box opens (**Figure 4.12**). In the **Start – Step 1 – Product** dialog box, by default the **Product** option, which creates a new product, is selected in the **Favorites** group. We continue with the default settings in the **Start – Step 1 – Product** dialog box.

2. *Click* the **Next** button to continue, as shown in **Figure 4.12**:

FIGURE 4.12

The **Start – Step 1 – Product** dialog box closes, and the **Product/Product DS** dialog box opens (**Figure 4.13**).

3. *Enter* a name for the assembly in the **Part Number** text box (**Figure 4.13**). In our case, we have entered **Product**.

4. *Click* the **Finish** button to close the **Product/Product DS** dialog box, as shown in **Figure 4.13**:

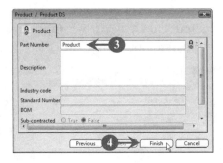

FIGURE 4.13

The **Product** assembly is created in the Assembly Design workbench, as shown in **Figure 4.14**:

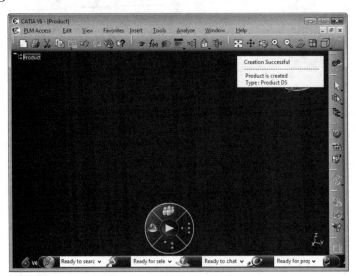

FIGURE 4.14

5. *Right-click* the **Product** assembly in the specification tree and *select* **Insert>Existing Representation** from the context menu, as shown in **Figure 4.15**:

FIGURE 4.15

The **Select representations to insert** dialog box opens (**Figure 4.16**).

6. *Select* the **From Session** tab to open the page associated with this tab (Figure 4.16).

7. *Click* the **Retrieve Loaded Data** button, as shown in Figure 4.16:

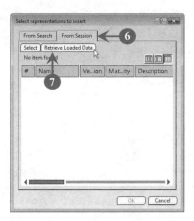

FIGURE 4.16

This displays all four components, **Part1**, **Part2**, **Part3**, and **Part4**, in the **Select representations to insert** dialog box (**Figure 4.17**).

8. *Select* the first component, **Part1** (Figure 4.17).

9. *Click* the **OK** button to close the **Select representations to insert** dialog box, as shown in Figure 4.17:

FIGURE 4.17

The **Part1** component is added to the **Product** assembly, as shown in **Figure 4.18**:

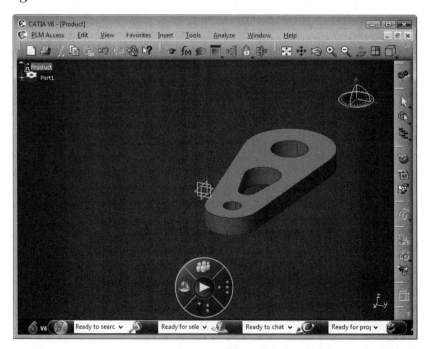

FIGURE 4.18

10. *Repeat* steps 5 to 9 to add the second component, **Part2**, to the **Product** assembly, as shown in **Figure 4.19**:

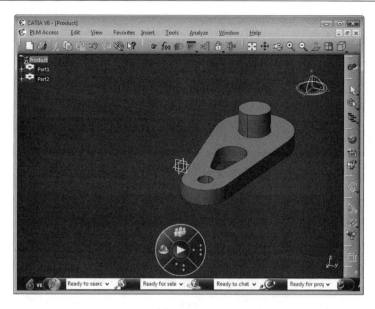

FIGURE 4.19

11. *Repeat* steps 5 to 9 to add the third component, **Part3**, to the **Product** assembly, as shown in **Figure 4.20**:

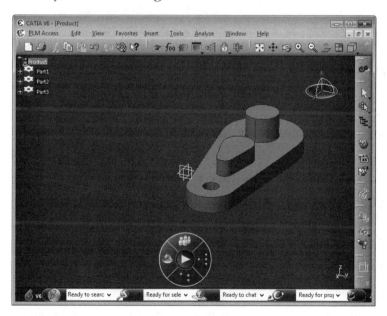

FIGURE 4.20

12. *Repeat* steps 5 to 9 to add the fourth component, **Part4**, to the **Product** assembly, as shown in **Figure 4.21**:

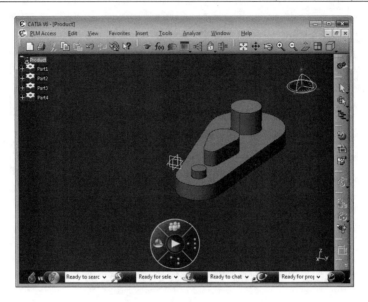

FIGURE 4.21

You have learned how to create an assembly. We next learn how to work with assembly components.

4.2 WORKING WITH ASSEMBLY COMPONENTS

After you create an assembly, you can still work with individual assembly components, such as replacing an assembly component with another component, and showing and hiding assembly components.

In this section, you learn to perform the following operations on the assembly components:

- Replacing assembly components
- Showing and hiding assembly components

We next begin with replacing assembly components.

Replacing Assembly Components

CATIA V6 allows you to replace an existing assembly component with a new assembly component. For this purpose, you need to first create a new assembly component and then replace the existing assembly component with the newly created assembly component. While creating a new component to replace an existing assembly component, you need to ensure that the new component has the same basic geometry as that of the original component. In such case, the new component is placed at the same location inside the assembly where the original component was placed. Otherwise, the new component should be placed at a different location.

Perform the following steps to learn how to replace an assembly component:

1. *Create* an assembly in the Assembly Design workbench, as shown in **Figure 4.22**:

FIGURE 4.22

2. *Select* **Start>Mechanical Design>Part Design** on the CATIA V6 user interface to start the Part Design workbench, as shown in **Figure 4.23**:

FIGURE 4.23

The **3D Shape/Representation DS** dialog box opens (**Figure 4.24**).

3. *Enter* a name for the new component in the **Representation Name** text box (Figure 4.24). In our case, we have entered **NewPart**.

4. *Click* the **Finish** button to close the **3D Shape/Representation DS** dialog box, as shown in Figure 4.24:

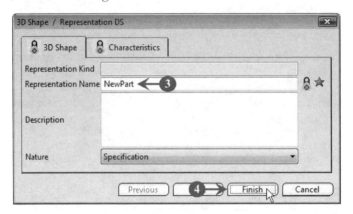

FIGURE 4.24

The **NewPart** component is created in the Part Design workbench (**Figure 4.25**). Now, you need to draw the sketch of the new component using the Sketcher workbench.

5. *Click* the **Sketch** button on the **Sketcher** toolbar (**Figure 4.25**).

6. *Select* the **xy-plane** option in the specification tree, as shown in Figure 4.25:

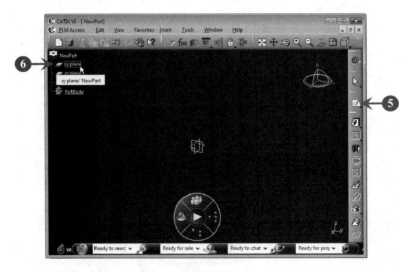

FIGURE 4.25

The Sketcher workbench gets displayed with the *xy*-plane as the sketching plane (**Figure 4.26**).

7. *Draw* a sketch in the Sketcher workbench (Figure 4.26).

8. *Click* the **Exit workbench** button on the Workbench toolbar to exit the Sketcher workbench, as shown in Figure 4.26:

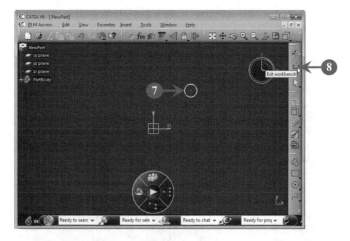

FIGURE 4.26

The Sketcher workbench closes and the Part Design workbench gets displayed (**Figure 4.27**).

9. *Select* **Insert>Sketch-Based Features>Pad** on the menu bar to apply the pad feature to the sketch that you have drawn in the Sketcher workbench, as shown in Figure 4.27:

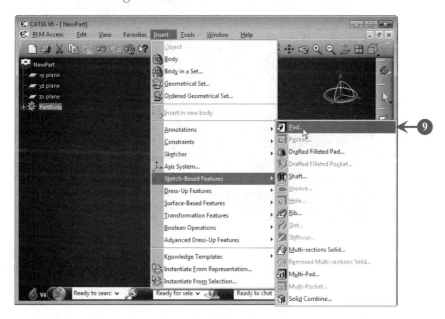

FIGURE 4.27

The **Pad Definition** dialog box opens and the sketch is turned into a solid model (**Figure 4.28**).

10. *Enter* **50 mm** in the **Length** box in the **First Limit** group (Figure 4.28).

11. *Click* the **OK** button to close the **Pad Definition** dialog box, as shown in Figure 4.28:

FIGURE 4.28

The new component for the assembly is created, as shown in **Figure 4.29**:

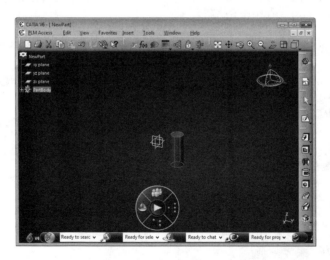

FIGURE 4.29

12. *Select* **Window>Product** from the menu bar, as shown in **Figure 4.30**:

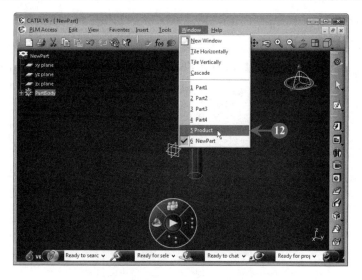

FIGURE 4.30

The Assembly Design workbench is displayed (**Figure 4.31**).

13. *Right-click* **Part4** in the specification tree and *select* **Replace>By Existing** from the context menu, as shown in Figure 4.31:

FIGURE 4.31

Note: You can delete an assembly component by *right-clicking* the component in the specification tree and selecting the **Delete** option from the context menu.

The **Replace Component** dialog box opens (**Figure 4.32**).

14. *Select* the **From Session** tab (Figure 4.32).
15. *Click* the **Retrieve Loaded Data** button, as shown in Figure 4.32:

FIGURE 4.32

This displays all four existing assembly components, **Part1**, **Part2**, **Part3**, and **Part4**, along with the **NewPart** component (**Figure 4.33**).

16. *Select* the **NewPart** component (Figure 4.33).
17. *Click* the **OK** button to close the **Replace Component** dialog box, as shown in Figure 4.33:

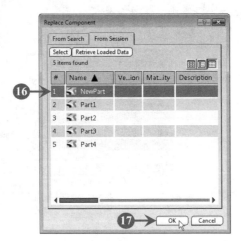

FIGURE 4.33

This replaces the existing assembly component, **Part4**, with the new component, **NewPart**, as shown in **Figure 4.34**:

FIGURE 4.34

You have learned how to replace the assembly components. We next learn how to show and hide assembly components.

Showing and Hiding Assembly Components

You can show or hide components in an assembly without permanently deleting the components from the assembly. Perform the following steps to show and hide components in an assembly:

1. *Create* an assembly in the Assembly Design workbench (**Figure 4.35**).
2. *Right-click* the assembly component that you want to hide in the specification tree and *select* the **Hide/Show** option from the context menu, as shown in Figure 4.35:

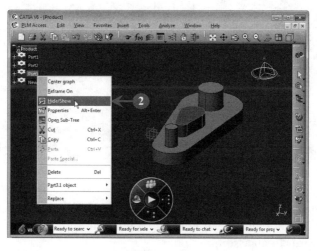

FIGURE 4.35

The selected assembly component is hidden (**Figure 4.36**).

3. Now, *right-click* the assembly component in the specification tree and *select* the **Hide/Show** option from the context menu to show the assembly component again, as shown in Figure 4.36:

FIGURE 4.36

The assembly component is displayed, as shown in **Figure 4.37**:

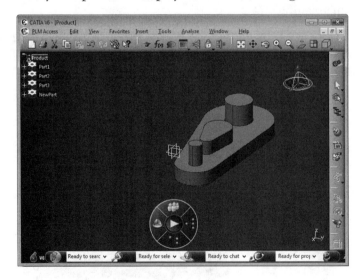

FIGURE 4.37

In this section, you have learned to replace an assembly component. You have also learned to show and hide an assembly component. The next section discusses how to use assembly features in an assembly.

4.3 USING ASSEMBLY FEATURES

The Assembly Design workbench enables you to edit and modify an assembly by providing some features, known as assembly features. These features include the hole feature, the protected feature, and the spilt feature. You can use these features to create an assembly hole, an assembly protected, and an assembly split. In this section, you learn how to use the following three assembly features:

- The hole feature
- The protected feature
- The split feature

Using the Hole Feature

You can use the hole feature to create an assembly hole in an assembly component. While creating an assembly hole, you need to specify dimensions for the hole. When you use the hole feature, a new product is created in the specification tree and a link is created between this new product and the component of the assembly where you want to create a hole.

Perform the following steps to use the hole feature:

1. *Create* an assembly in the Assembly Design workbench, as shown in **Figure 4.38**:

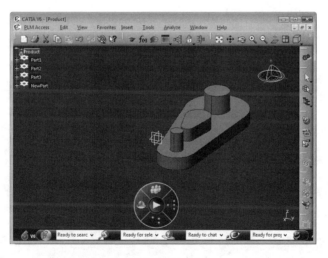

FIGURE 4.38

2. *Select* **Insert>Assembly Features>Hole** from the menu bar, as shown in **Figure 4.39**:

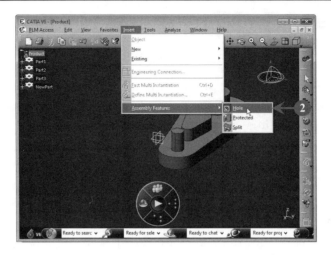

FIGURE 4.39

3. *Click* the **Launch Assembly Feature Definition** button on the **Creation** toolbar to prevent the **Assembly Feature Definition** dialog box from appearing at the end of hole creation (**Figure 4.40**).

4. *Click* the **Specification in No Show** button on the **Creation** toolbar to show the hole at the end of its creation (Figure 4.40).

5. *Select* the component of the assembly in which you want to create a hole, as shown in Figure 4.40:

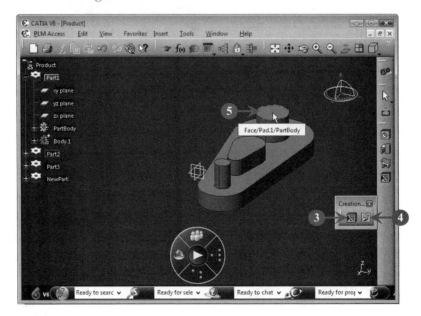

FIGURE 4.40

The **Body.1** product is created in the specification tree (Figure 4.40), and a warning message indicating that a link is about to be created between the new product and the selected component of the assembly, is displayed (**Figure 4.41**).

6. *Click* the **OK** button to close the message box, as shown in Figure 4.41:

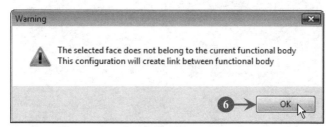

FIGURE 4.41

The **Hole Definition** dialog box opens (**Figure 4.42**).

7. *Specify* the options, such as diameter and depth of the hole, in the **Hole Definition** dialog box (Figure 4.42). In our case, we have just changed the depth of the hole in the **Depth** text box from **10 mm** to **50 mm**.

8. *Click* the **OK** button to close the **Hole Definition** dialog box, as shown in Figure 4.42:

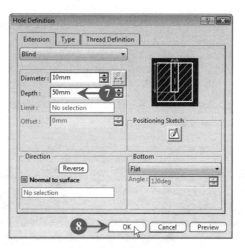

FIGURE 4.42

A hole with the specified properties is created in the selected assembly component, as shown in **Figure 4.43**:

FIGURE 4.43

After learning how to use the hole feature, we next learn how to use the protected feature.

Using the Protected Feature

You can use the protected feature to create an assembly protected on an assembly component. An assembly protected is a structure built on a component of an assembly and it can be any of the shapes, such as a prism, a sweep, and a revolve.

Perform the following steps to use the protected feature:

1. *Create* an assembly in the Assembly Design workbench (**Figure 4.44**).
2. *Select* **Insert>Assembly Features>Protected** from the menu bar, as shown in Figure 4.44:

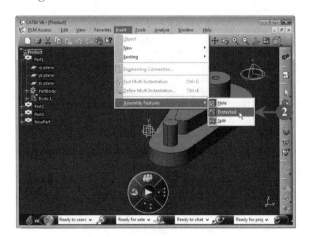

FIGURE 4.44

The **Protected Feature** dialog box appears (**Figure 4.45**).

3. *Click* the **Launch Assembly Feature Definition** button on the **Creation** toolbar to prevent the **Assembly Feature Definition** dialog box from appearing at the end of the creation of assembly protected (Figure 4.45).

4. *Click* the **Specification in No Show** button on the **Creation** toolbar to show the assembly protected at the end of its creation (Figure 4.45).

5. *Select* the component of the assembly in which you want to create an assembly protected, as shown in Figure 4.45:

FIGURE 4.45

The selected surface of the component is added to the **Profile/Surface** box in the **Protected Feature** dialog box and also displays a preview of the assembly protected (**Figure 4.46**).

6. *Click* the **OK** button to close the **Protected Feature** dialog box, as shown in Figure 4.46:

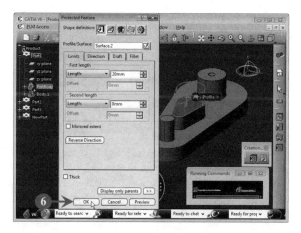

FIGURE 4.46

An assembly protected is created on the selected assembly component, as shown in **Figure 4.47**:

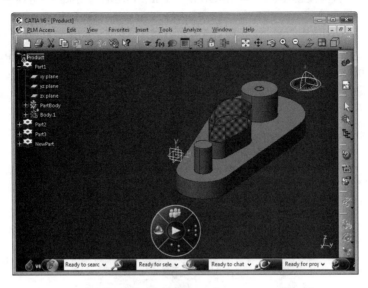

FIGURE 4.47

Using the Split Feature

The split feature allows you to create an assembly split (cut) in an assembly. You can use this feature to remove an assembly hole or assembly protected from an assembly.

Perform the following steps to use the split feature:

1. *Create* an assembly in the Assembly Design workbench (**Figure 4.48**).
2. *Select* **Insert > Assembly Features > Split** from the menu bar, as shown in Figure 4.48:

FIGURE 4.48

The **Cut** dialog box opens (**Figure 4.49**).

3. *Click* the **Launch Assembly Feature Definition** button on the **Creation** toolbar to prevent the **Assembly Feature Definition** dialog box from appearing at the end of the split operation (Figure 4.49).

4. *Click* the **Specification in No Show** button on the **Creation** toolbar to show the result of the split operation (Figure 4.49).

5. *Select* the assembly feature that you want to cut, as shown in Figure 4.49:

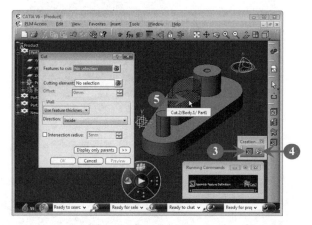

FIGURE 4.49

The selected feature is added to the **Features to cut** box in the **Cut** dialog box (**Figure 4.50**).

6. *Select* the component from which you want to remove the feature, as shown in Figure 4.50:

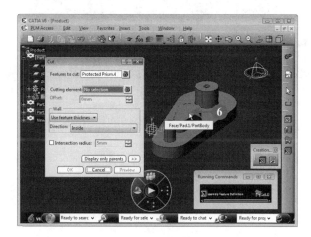

FIGURE 4.50

The selected surface of the component is added to the **Features to cut** box in the **Cut** dialog box (**Figure 4.51**).

7.   *Click* the **OK** button to close the **Cut** dialog box, as shown in Figure 4.51:

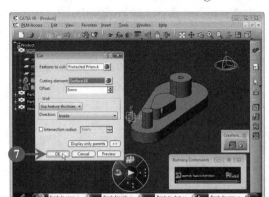

FIGURE 4.51

The selected assembly feature is removed, as shown in **Figure 4.52**:

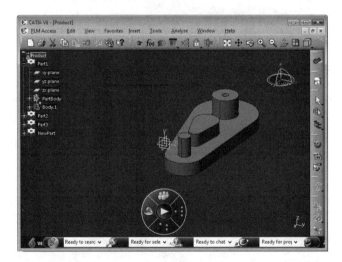

FIGURE 4.52

We next summarize the main topics covered in this chapter.

SUMMARY

In this chapter, you have learned how to

- Create an assembly
- Work with assembly components
- Use assembly features

WIREFRAME AND SURFACE DESIGN WORKBENCH

Chapter **5**

The Wireframe and Surface Design workbench of CATIA V6 allows you to create wireframe elements and surfaces. Wireframe elements are sketches used to create surfaces, which are three-dimensional (3D) models without any thickness and mass properties. The process of creating surfaces is known as surface modeling. The Wireframe and Surface Design workbench provides a number of options for surface modeling that helps in product styling by providing a unique shape to the product components. These options also help to make the product more attractive and presentable.

This chapter helps you learn how to create wireframe elements and surfaces. First, you learn how to create different wireframe elements, such as a point, line, plane, and circle. After that, the creation of different types of surfaces, such as an extruded surface, revolved surface, spherical surface, cylindrical surface, offset surface, swept surface, fill surface, and multi-sections surface, is discussed.

We begin with creating wireframe elements.

5.1 CREATING WIREFRAME ELEMENTS

The Wireframe and Surface Design workbench provides options to create sketches, known as wireframe elements. Examples of wireframe elements are a point, line, plane, and circle. Using the wireframe elements, you can draw sketches to create surfaces in the Wireframe and Surface Design workbench instead of the Sketcher workbench.

Alternatively, you can invoke the Sketcher workbench from the Wireframe and Surface Design workbench to draw sketches for your surfaces, and then exit the Sketcher workbench and return back to the Wireframe and Surface Design workbench.

In this section, you learn to create the following four wireframe elements:

- Point
- Line
- Plane
- Circle

We begin with creating a point.

Creating a Point

While creating a point in the Wireframe and Surface Design workbench, you need to specify all three coordinates (x-coordinate, y-coordinate, and z-coordinate) for the point to be created. The point created in the Wireframe and Surface Design workbench is represented with a cross sign (×) instead of the plus sign (+), which is used to represent a point in the Sketcher workbench.

Perform the following steps to create a point in the Wireframe and Surface Design workbench:

1. *Open* CATIA V6.
2. *Select* **Start>Mechanical Design>Wireframe and Surface Design** on the CATIA V6 user interface to start the Wireframe and Surface Design workbench, as shown in **Figure 5.1**:

FIGURE 5.1

The **3D Shape/Representation DS** dialog box opens (**Figure 5.2**).

3. *Enter* a name for the representation in the **Representation Name** text box (Figure 5.2). In our case, we continue with the default name, **Representation1**.

4. *Click* the **Finish** button to close the **3D Shape/Representation DS** dialog box, as shown in Figure 5.2:

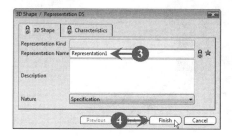

FIGURE 5.2

The **Representation1** representation is created in the Wireframe and Surface Design workbench, as shown in **Figure 5.3**:

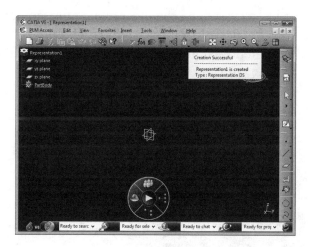

FIGURE 5.3

5. *Select* **Insert>Wireframe>Point** from the menu bar to create a point, as shown in **Figure 5.4**:

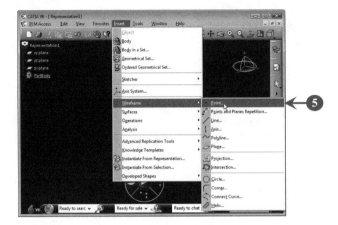

FIGURE 5.4

The **Point Definition** dialog box opens (**Figure 5.5**).

6. *Enter* a value representing the *x*-coordinate for the point in the **X =** box (Figure 5.5). In our case, we have entered **10 mm**.

7. *Enter* a value representing the *y*-coordinate for the point in the **Y =** box (Figure 5.5). In our case, we have entered **20 mm**.

8. *Enter* a value representing the *z*-coordinate for the point in the **Z =** box (Figure 5.5). In our case, we have entered **30 mm**.

9. *Click* the **OK** button to close the **Point Definition** dialog box, as shown in Figure 5.5:

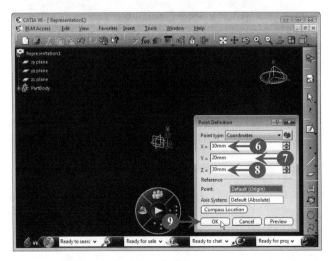

FIGURE 5.5

A point is created, as shown in **Figure 5.6**:

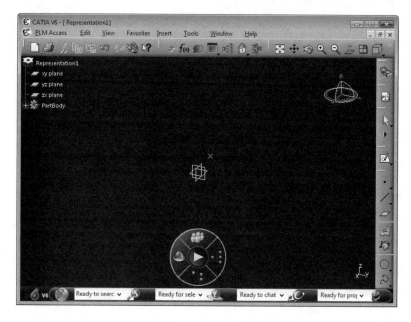

FIGURE 5.6

You learned how to create a point in the Wireframe and Surface Design workbench. We next learn how to create a line in the Wireframe and Surface Design workbench.

Creating a Line

You can create a line in the Wireframe and Surface Design workbench either by creating the starting and ending points for the line or by selecting two existing points as the starting and ending points for the line.

Perform the following steps to create a line in the Wireframe and Surface Design workbench:

1. *Start* the Wireframe and Surface Design workbench.

2.   *Select* **Insert>Wireframe>Line** from the menu bar to create a line, as shown in **Figure 5.7**:

FIGURE 5.7

The **Line Definition** dialog box opens (**Figure 5.8**).

3.   *Right-click* inside the **Point 1** box and *select* the **Insert Wireframe>Create Point** option from the context menu, as shown in Figure 5.8:

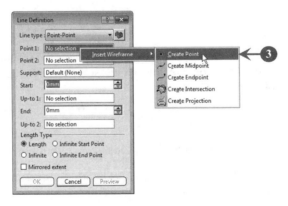

FIGURE 5.8

The **Point Definition** dialog box opens (**Figure 5.9**).

4.   *Enter* a value representing the x-coordinate for the starting point of the line in the **X =** box (Figure 5.9). In our case, we have entered **10 mm**.

5. *Enter* a value representing the *y*-coordinate for the starting point of the line in the **Y =** box (Figure 5.9). In our case, we have entered **20 mm**.

6. *Enter* a value representing the *z*-coordinate for the starting point of the line in the **Z =** box (Figure 5.9). In our case, we have entered **30 mm**.

7. *Click* the **OK** button to close the **Point Definition** dialog box, as shown in Figure 5.9:

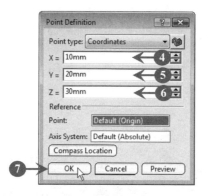

FIGURE 5.9

The starting point for the line is added to the **Point 1** box (**Figure 5.10**).

8. *Right-click* inside the **Point 2** box and *select* the **Insert Wireframe>Create Point** option from the context menu, as shown in Figure 5.10:

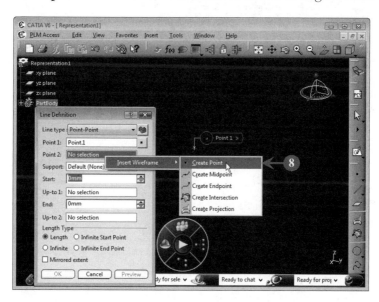

FIGURE 5.10

The **Point Definition** dialog box opens (**Figure 5.11**).

9. *Enter* a value representing the x-coordinate for the end point of the line in the **X =** box (Figure 5.11). In our case, we have entered **10 mm**.

10. *Enter* a value representing the y-coordinate for the end point of the line in the **Y =** box (Figure 5.11). In our case, we have entered **50 mm**.

11. *Enter* a value representing the z-coordinate for the end point of the line in the **Z =** box (Figure 5.11). In our case, we have entered **80 mm** (to view the change in the value of the **Z =** box, click any option in the **Point Definition** dialog box).

12. *Click* the **OK** button to close the **Point Definition** dialog box, as shown in Figure 5.11:

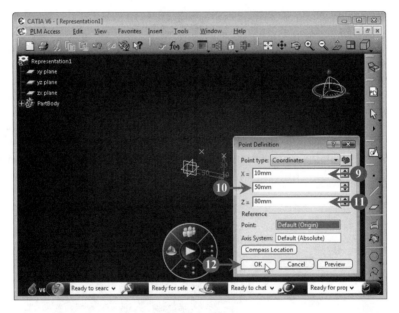

FIGURE 5.11

The end point for the line is added to the **Point 2** box in the **Line Definition** dialog box (**Figure 5.12**).

13. *Click* the **OK** button to close the **Line Definition** dialog box, as shown in Figure 5.12:

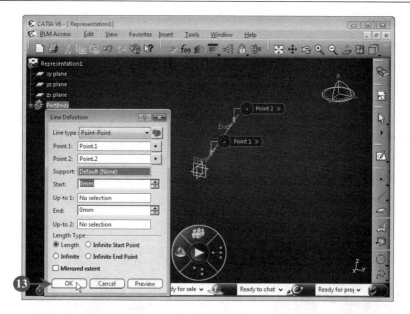

FIGURE 5.12

A line is created, as shown in **Figure 5.13**:

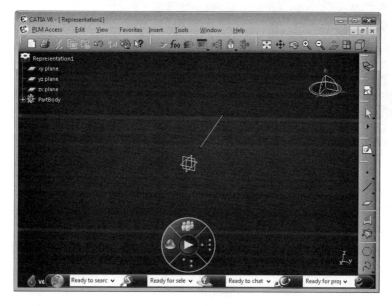

FIGURE 5.13

The next section discusses how to create a plane in the Wireframe and Surface Design workbench.

Creating a Plane

By default, the CATIA V6 user interface displays three planes: *xy*, *yz*, and *zx*. In addition to these three default planes, the Wireframe and Surface Design workbench of CATIA V6 allows you to create additional planes by taking any of these planes as the reference plane. You generally need to create an additional plane while drawing a sketch relative to an already drawn sketch. Such planes help to give a more exact and appropriate shape to your surfaces.

Perform the following steps to create a plane:

1. *Start* the Wireframe and Surface Design workbench.

2. *Select* **Insert > Wireframe > Plane** from the menu bar to create a plane, as shown in **Figure 5.14**:

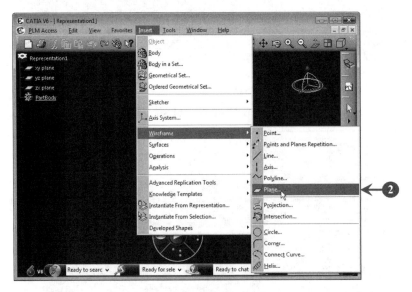

FIGURE 5.14

The **Plane Definition** dialog box opens (**Figure 5.15**).

3. *Right-click* inside the **Reference** box and *select* the **Insert Wireframe > XY-Plane** option from the context menu to specify the *xy*-plane as the reference plane for the plane to be created, as shown in Figure 5.15:

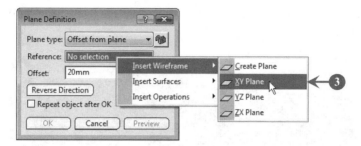

FIGURE 5.15

Note: You can also specify *yz* and *zx*-planes as the reference planes for a plane by *right-clicking* inside the **Reference** box in the **Plane Definition** dialog box and selecting the **Insert Wireframe>YZ-Plane** and **Insert Wireframe>ZX-Plane** options, respectively, from the context menu.

The reference plane is added to the **Reference** box in the **Plane Definition** dialog box (**Figure 5.16**).

4. *Enter* a value representing the offset from the reference plane in the **Offset** box (Figure 5.16). In our case, we have entered **50 mm**.

5. *Click* the **OK** button to close the **Plane Definition** dialog box, as shown in Figure 5.16:

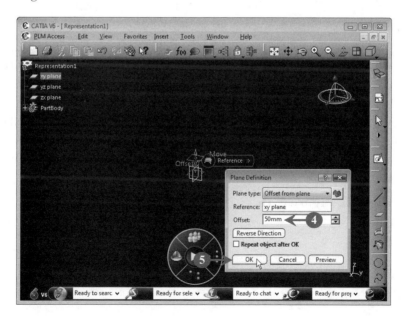

FIGURE 5.16

A plane is created at an offset of 50 mm from the xy-plane, as shown in **Figure 5.17**:

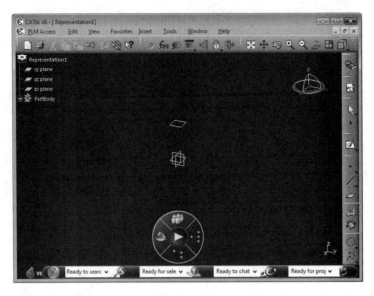

FIGURE 5.17

After learning to create a point, line, and a plane, we next learn how to create another wireframe element, a circle.

Creating a Circle

A circle is generally a part of the sketch for a surface. You can create a circle in the Wireframe and Surface Design workbench by specifying the center, the radius, and a plane as the support surface for the circle. The center for a circle can be specified by either creating a new point or selecting an existing point.

Perform the following steps to create a circle in the Wireframe and Surface Design workbench:

1. *Start* the Wireframe and Surface Design workbench.
2. *Select* **Insert > Wireframe > Circle** from the menu bar to create a circle, as shown in **Figure 5.18**:

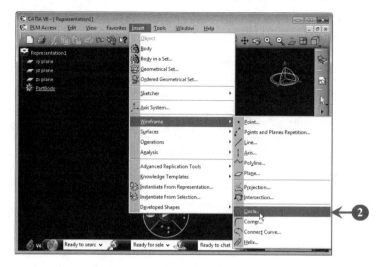

FIGURE 5.18

The **Circle Definition** dialog box opens (**Figure 5.19**).

3. *Right-click* inside the **Center** box and *select* the **Insert Wireframe>Create Point** option from the context menu to create the center of the circle, as shown in Figure 5.19:

FIGURE 5.19

The **Point Definition** dialog box opens (**Figure 5.20**).

4. *Enter* a value representing the *x*-coordinate for the center of the circle in the **X =** box (Figure 5.20). In our case, we have entered **10 mm**.

5. *Enter* a value representing the *y*-coordinate for the center of the circle in the **Y =** box (Figure 5.20). In our case, we have entered **10 mm**.

6. *Enter* a value representing the *z*-coordinate for the center of the circle in the **Z =** box (Figure 5.20). In our case, we have entered **50 mm**.

7. *Click* the **OK** button to close the **Point Definition** dialog box, as shown in Figure 5.20:

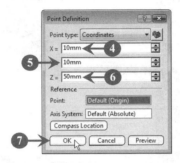

FIGURE 5.20

The center of the circle is added to the **Center** box in the **Circle Definition** dialog box (**Figure 5.21**).

8. *Right-click* inside the **Support** box and *select* the **Insert Wireframe > XY-Plane** option from the context menu to select the *xy*-plane as the support surface for the circle, as shown in Figure 5.21:

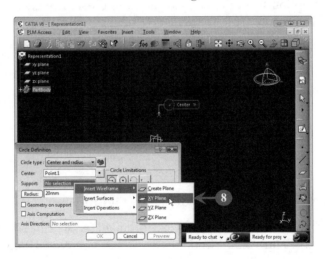

FIGURE 5.21

The support surface is added to the **Support** box in the **Circle Definition** dialog box (**Figure 5.22**).

9. *Enter* a value representing the radius of the circle in the box beside the **Radius** button (Figure 5.22). In our case, we have entered **30 mm**.

10. *Enter* **360deg** in the **End** box in the **Circle Limitations** group (Figure 5.22).

11. *Click* the **OK** button to close the **Circle Definition** dialog box, as shown in Figure 5.22:

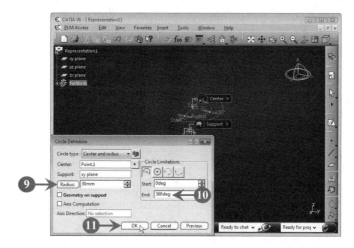

FIGURE 5.22

A circle is created, as shown in **Figure 5.23**:

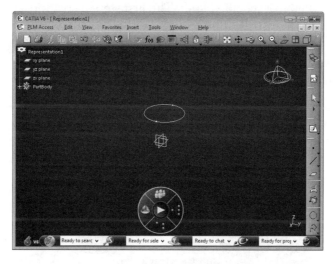

FIGURE 5.23

You learned how to create wireframe elements. The next section discusses how to create surfaces.

5.2 CREATING SURFACES

A surface or a surface model is a 3D model having negligible thickness. The Wireframe and Surface Design workbench allows you to create surfaces by performing different operations, such as extruding, revolving, sweeping, and filling on a profile. This workbench also allows you to create spherical, cylindrical, offset, and multi-section surfaces.

In this section, you learn to create the following surfaces:

- Extruded surface
- Revolved surface
- Spherical surface
- Cylindrical surface
- Offset surface
- Swept surface
- Fill surface
- Multi-section surface

Let's discuss each of these one by one.

Creating an Extruded Surface

An extruded surface is a surface that is created by extruding a profile (sketch) along with a specified direction up to a specified limit. The first step in creating an extruded surface is to create the profile to extrude. Once you have created the profile, you can create the extruded surface by specifying parameters, such as the profile to be extruded, direction of extrusion, and extrusion limits.

Perform the following steps to create an extruded surface:

1. *Start* the Wireframe and Surface Design workbench.
2. *Select* **Insert > Surfaces > Extrude** from the menu bar to create the desired extruded surface, as shown in **Figure 5.24**:

FIGURE 5.24

The **Extruded Surface Definition** dialog box opens (**Figure 5.25**).

3. *Right-click* inside the **Profile** box and *select* the **Insert Wireframe>Create Sketch** option from the context menu to create the sketch of the surface, as shown in Figure 5.25:

FIGURE 5.25

4. *Select* the **xy-plane** option in the specification tree to invoke the Sketcher workbench with the *xy*-plane as the sketching plane, as shown in **Figure 5.26**:

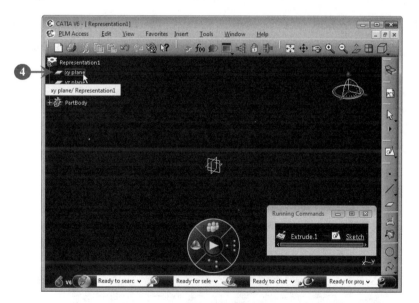

FIGURE 5.26

The Sketcher workbench is displayed with the *xy*-plane as the sketching plane (**Figure 5.27**).

5. *Select* **Insert > Profile > Spline > Spline** from the menu bar to draw a spline, as shown in Figure 5.27:

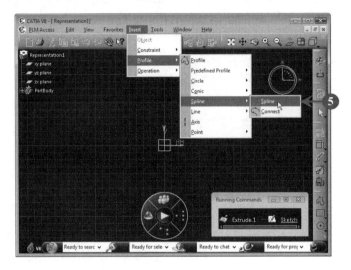

FIGURE 5.27

6. *Draw* a spline, which works as the profile to be extruded (**Figure 5.28**).

7. *Click* the **Exit workbench** button on the **Workbench** toolbar to exit the Sketcher workbench, as shown in Figure 5.28:

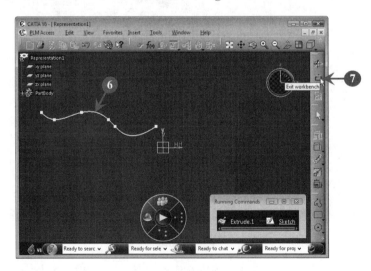

FIGURE 5.28

The Wireframe and Surface Design workbench reappears, and the sketch that you have just created and the sketching plane used to create the sketch is added to the **Profile** and **Direction** boxes, respectively, in the **Extruded Surface Definition** dialog box (**Figure 5.29**).

8. *Enter* a value representing the dimension for the surface to be created in the **Dimension** box under the **Limit 1** group in the **Extrusion Limits** group (Figure 5.29). In our case, we have entered **50 mm**.

9. *Click* the **OK** button to close the **Extruded Surface Definition** dialog box, as shown in Figure 5.29:

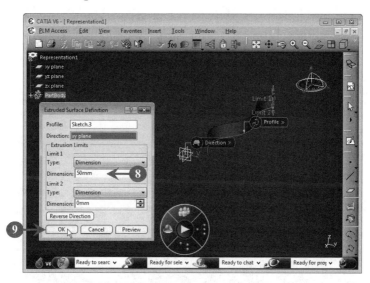

FIGURE 5.29

The resulting extruded surface is shown in **Figure 5.30**:

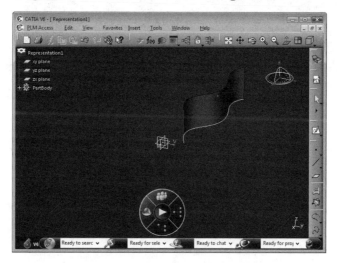

FIGURE 5.30

Creating a Revolved Surface

A revolved surface is a surface that is created by revolving a profile around an axis. The axis around which the profile is revolved is called a revolution axis. For creating a revolved surface, you need to create the profile to revolve and the revolution axis. After you have created the profile and the revolution axis, you can create the revolved surface by specifying parameters, such as the profile, revolution axis, and angle of revolution.

Perform the following steps to create a revolved surface:

1. *Start* the Wireframe and Surface Design workbench.
2. *Click* the **Sketch** button on the **Sketcher** toolbar to draw the sketch of the profile (**Figure 5.31**).
3. *Select* the **zx-plane** option in the specification tree to invoke the Sketcher workbench with the *zx*-plane as the sketching plane, as shown in Figure 5.31:

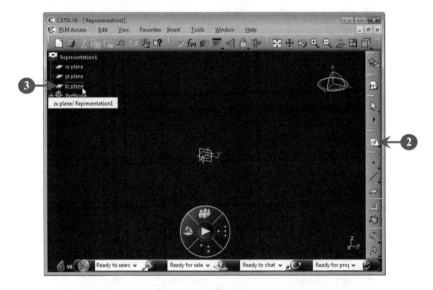

FIGURE 5.31

The Sketcher workbench is displayed with the *zx*-plane as the sketching plane (**Figure 5.32**).

4. *Select* **Insert > Profile > Spline > Spline** from the menu bar to draw a spline, as shown in Figure 5.32:

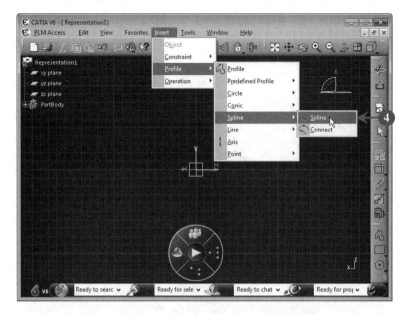

FIGURE 5.32

5. *Draw* a spline, which works as the profile to be revolved, as shown in **Figure 5.33**:

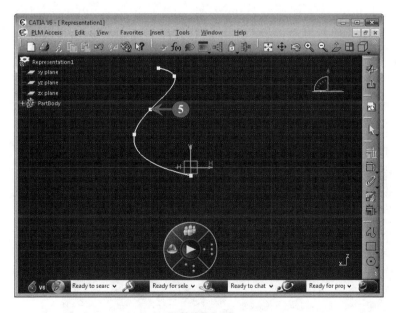

FIGURE 5.33

6. *Select* **Insert** > **Profile** > **Axis** from the menu bar to draw the revolution axis, as shown in **Figure 5.34**:

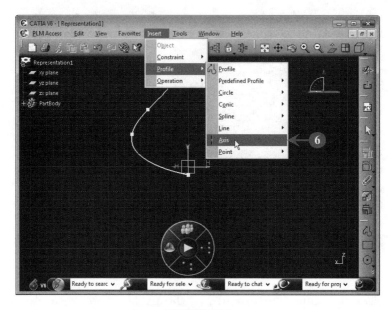

FIGURE 5.34

7. *Draw* an axis parallel to the z axis that is the revolution axis (**Figure 5.35**).

8. *Click* the **Exit workbench** button on the **Workbench** toolbar to exit the Sketcher workbench, as shown in Figure 5.35:

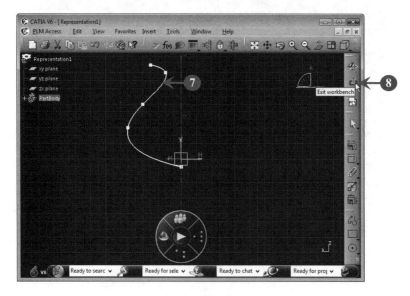

FIGURE 5.35

Figure 5.36 shows the sketch of the revolved surface to be created in the Wireframe and Surface Design workbench:

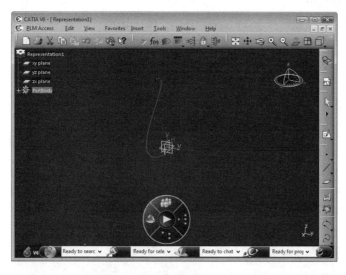

FIGURE 5.36

9. *Select* **Insert > Surfaces > Revolve** from the menu bar to create the desired revolved surface, as shown in **Figure 5.37**:

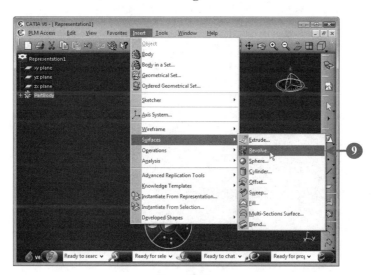

FIGURE 5.37

The **Revolution Surface Definition** dialog box opens with the profile and the revolution axis automatically added to the **Profile** and **Revolution axis** boxes, respectively (**Figure 5.38**).

10. *Enter* a value representing the angle of revolution in the **Angle 1** box in the **Angular Limits** group (Figure 5.38). In our case, we have entered **360deg**.

11. *Click* the **OK** button to close the **Revolution Surface Definition** dialog box, as shown in Figure 5.38:

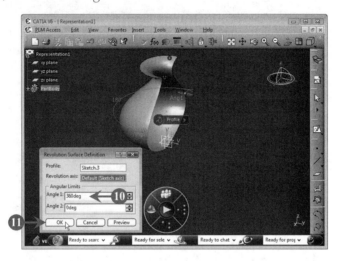

FIGURE 5.38

The resulting revolved surface is shown in **Figure 5.39**:

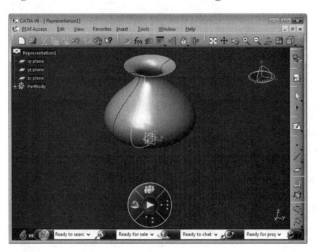

FIGURE 5.39

Creating a Spherical Surface

A spherical surface is a surface that has a shape similar to a sphere. You can create a spherical surface in the Wireframe and Surface Design workbench by specifying the center and the radius for the circle and an axis system as the sphere axis. By default, the axis system (xyz) is selected as the sphere axis. You can either create a new point or specify an existing point as the center of the spherical surface.

Perform the following steps to create a spherical surface:

1. *Start* the Wireframe and Surface Design workbench.

2. *Select* **Insert > Surfaces > Sphere** from the menu bar to create the desired spherical surface, as shown in **Figure 5.40**:

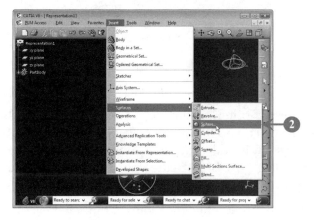

FIGURE 5.40

The **Sphere Surface Definition** dialog box opens (**Figure 5.41**).

3. *Right-click* inside the **Center** box and *select* the **Insert Wireframe > Create Point** option from the context menu to create the center for the spherical surface, as shown in Figure 5.41:

FIGURE 5.41

The **Point Definition** dialog box opens (**Figure 5.42**).

4. *Enter* a value representing the *x*-coordinate for the center of the spherical surface in the **X =** box (Figure 5.42). In our case, we have entered **10 mm**.

5. *Enter* a value representing the *y*-coordinate for the center of the spherical surface in the **Y =** box (Figure 5.42). In our case, we have entered **20 mm**.

6. *Enter* a value representing the *z*-coordinate for the center of the spherical surface in the **Z =** box (Figure 5.42). In our case, we have entered **30 mm**.

7. *Click* the **OK** button to close the **Point Definition** dialog box, as shown in Figure 5.42:

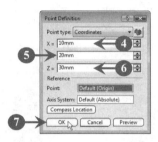

FIGURE 5.42

The center for the spherical surface is created and added to the **Center** box in the **Sphere Surface Definition** dialog box (**Figure 5.43**). Notice that the default axis system is added to the **Sphere axis** box in the **Sphere Surface Definition** dialog box. In our case, we continue with the default value for the sphere axis.

8. *Enter* a value representing the radius of the spherical surface in the **Sphere radius** box (Figure 5.43). In our case, we have entered **50 mm**.

9. *Click* the **Create the whole sphere** button to create the complete sphere, as shown in Figure 5.43:

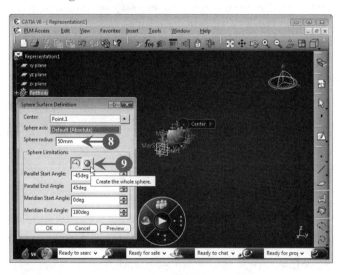

FIGURE 5.43

10. *Click* the **OK** button to close the **Sphere Surface Definition** dialog box, as shown in **Figure 5.44**:

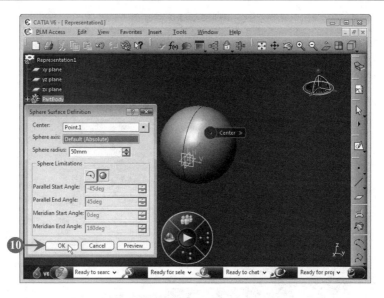

FIGURE 5.44

The resulting spherical surface is shown in **Figure 5.45**:

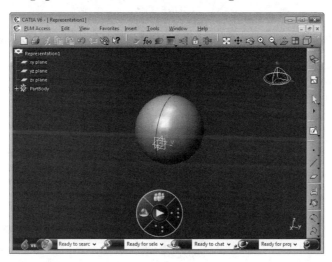

FIGURE 5.45

Creating a Cylindrical Surface

A cylindrical surface is a surface that has a shape similar to a cylinder. You can create a cylindrical surface in the Wireframe and Surface Design workbench by specifying parameters, such as the center, radius, and height (depth) of the cylindrical surface and the direction in which the cylindrical surface is created.

Perform the following steps to create a cylindrical surface:

1. *Start* the Wireframe and Surface Design workbench.
2. *Select* **Insert > Surfaces > Cylinder** from the menu bar to create the desired cylindrical surface, as shown in **Figure 5.46**:

FIGURE 5.46

The **Cylinder Surface Definition** dialog box opens (**Figure 5.47**).

3. *Right-click* inside the **Point** box and *select* the **Insert Wireframe > Create Point** option from the context menu to create the center for the cylindrical surface, as shown in Figure 5.47:

FIGURE 5.47

The **Point Definition** dialog box opens (Figure 5.48).

4. *Enter* a value representing the x-coordinate for the center of the cylindrical surface in the **X =** box (Figure 5.48). In our case, we have entered **10 mm**.
5. *Enter* a value representing the y-coordinate for the center of the cylindrical surface in the **Y =** box (Figure 5.48). In our case, we have entered **20 mm**.
6. *Enter* a value representing the z-coordinate for the center of the cylindrical surface in the **Z =** box (Figure 5.48). In our case, we have entered **30 mm**.

7. *Click* the **OK** button to close the **Point Definition** dialog box, as shown in Figure 5.48:

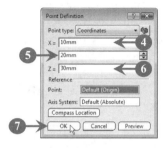

FIGURE 5.48

The center for the cylindrical surface is created and added to the **Point** box in the **Cylinder Surface Definition** dialog box (**Figure 5.49**).

8. *Right-click* inside the **Direction** box and *select* the **Z Component** option from the context menu to specify the *z*-axis as the direction for the cylindrical surface, as shown in Figure 5.49:

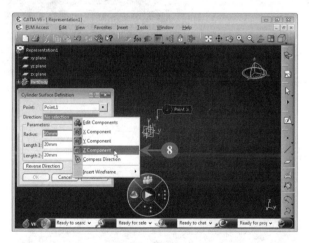

FIGURE 5.49

Note: You can also specify the *x*-axis or the *y*-axis as the direction for the cylindrical surface by *right-clicking* inside the **Direction** box in the **Cylinder Surface Definition** dialog box and selecting the **X Component** and **Y Component** options, respectively, from the context menu.

9. *Enter* a value representing the radius for the cylindrical surface in the **Radius** box in the **Parameters** group (**Figure 5.50**). In our case, we have entered **50 mm**.

10. *Enter* a value representing the height of the cylindrical surface with respect to the center of the cylindrical surface in the **Length 1** box in the **Parameters** group (Figure 5.50). In our case, we have entered **80 mm**.

11. *Enter* a value representing the depth of the cylindrical surface with respect to the center of the cylindrical surface in the **Length 2** box in the **Parameters** group (Figure 5.50). In our case, we continue with the default value, **20 mm**.

12. *Click* the **OK** button to close the **Cylinder Surface Definition** dialog box, as shown in Figure 5.50:

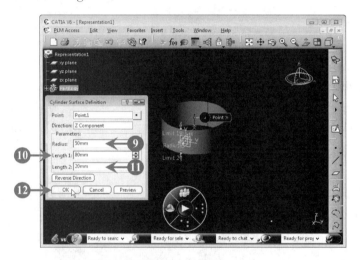

FIGURE 5.50

The resulting cylindrical surface is shown in **Figure 5.51**:

FIGURE 5.51

Creating an Offset Surface

The Wireframe and Surface Design workbench allows you to create a surface, called an offset surface, which is at an offset from a reference surface. The offset surface has the same shape and size as that of the reference surface. You can create an offset surface by first creating a reference surface; you can also use an already created surface as the reference surface. In our case, we first create the reference surface and then use this reference surface to create an offset surface.

Perform the following steps to create an offset surface:

1. *Start* the Wireframe and Surface Design workbench.
2. *Click* the **Sketch** button on the **Sketcher** toolbar to draw the sketch of the reference surface (**Figure 5.52**).
3. *Select* the **zx-plane** option in the specification tree to invoke the Sketcher workbench with the *zx*-plane as the sketching plane, as shown in Figure 5.52:

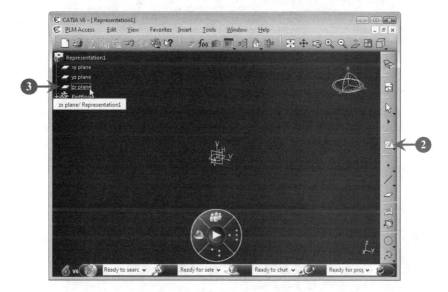

FIGURE 5.52

The Sketcher workbench is displayed with the *zx*-plane as the sketching plane (**Figure 5.53**).

4. *Select* **Insert** > **Profile** > **Line** > **Line** from the menu bar to draw a line, as shown in Figure 5.53:

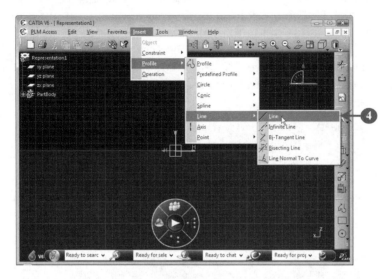

FIGURE 5.53

5. *Draw* a line, which works as the profile to be extruded to create the reference surface (**Figure 5.54**).
6. *Click* the **Exit workbench** button on the **Workbench** toolbar to exit the Sketcher workbench, as shown in Figure 5.54:

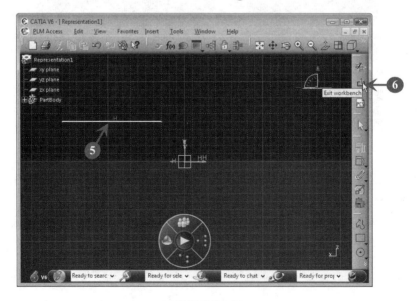

FIGURE 5.54

Figure 5.55 shows the sketch of the reference surface in the Wireframe and Surface Design workbench:

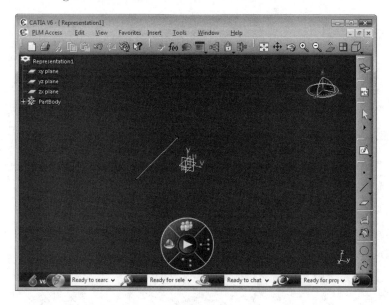

FIGURE 5.55

7. *Select* **Insert>Surfaces>Extrude** from the menu bar to create the reference surface, as shown in **Figure 5.56**:

FIGURE 5.56

The **Extruded Surface Definition** dialog box opens (**Figure 5.57**).

8. *Select* the profile to be extruded, as shown in Figure 5.57:

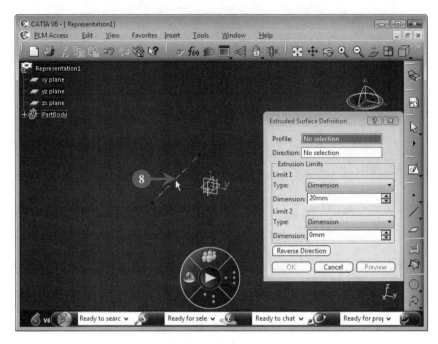

FIGURE 5.57

The selected profile and the reference plane are added to the **Profile** and **Direction** boxes, respectively, in the **Extruded Surface Definition** dialog box (**Figure 5.58**).

9. *Enter* a value representing the length of the surface in the right direction, in the **Dimension** box under the **Limit 1** group in the **Extrusion Limits** group (Figure 5.58). In our case, we have entered **50 mm**.
10. *Enter* a value representing the length of the surface in the left direction, in the **Dimension** box under the **Limit 2** group in the **Extrusion Limits** group (Figure 5.58). In our case, we continue with the default value, **0 mm**.
11. *Click* the **OK** button to close the **Extruded Surface Definition** dialog box, as shown in Figure 5.58:

FIGURE 5.58

Figure 5.59 shows the resulting reference surface:

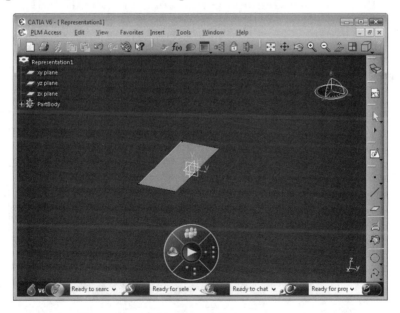

FIGURE 5.59

12. *Select* **Insert**>**Surfaces**>**Offset** from the menu bar to create the desired offset surface, as shown in **Figure 5.60**:

FIGURE 5.60

The **Offset Surface Definition** dialog box opens (**Figure 5.61**).

13. *Select* the reference surface, as shown in Figure 5.61:

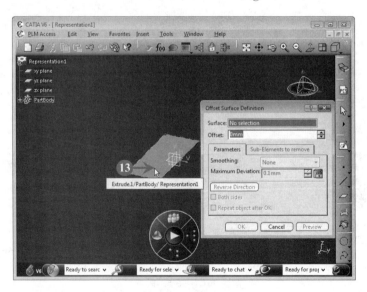

FIGURE 5.61

The selected reference surface is added to the **Surface** box in the **Offset Surface Definition** dialog box (**Figure 5.62**).

14. *Enter* a value representing the offset from the reference plane in the **Offset** box (Figure 5.62). In our case, we have entered **50 mm**.

15. *Click* the **OK** button to close the **Offset Surface Definition** dialog box, as shown in Figure 5.62:

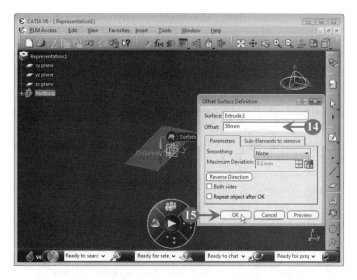

FIGURE 5.62

The resulting offset surface is shown in **Figure 5.63**:

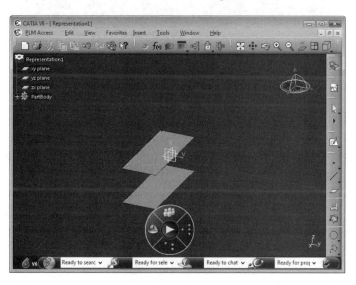

FIGURE 5.63

We next learn how to create swept surfaces.

Creating a Swept Surface

A swept surface is a surface that is created by sweeping a profile along a curve, known as a guide curve. You can create a swept surface by creating a guide curve and then creating a profile as two separate sketches. Once you have created a guide curve and the profile, you can create a swept surface. In our example, we first create a guide curve along which the profile can be swept, then create a plane that we use as the sketching plane to draw the profile, then draw the profile, and finally create the swept surface.

Perform the following steps to create a swept surface:

1. *Start* the Wireframe and Surface Design workbench.
2. *Click* the **Sketch** button on the **Sketcher** toolbar to draw the sketch of the guide curve of the desired swept surface (**Figure 5.64**).
3. *Select* the **xy-plane** option in the specification tree to invoke the Sketcher workbench with the *xy*-plane as the sketching plane, as shown in Figure 5.64:

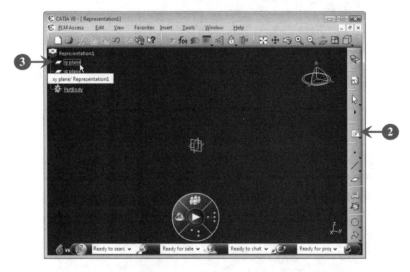

FIGURE 5.64

The Sketcher workbench is displayed with the *xy*-plane as the sketching plane (**Figure 5.65**).

4. *Select* **Insert** > **Profile** > **Spline** > **Spline** from the menu bar to draw a spline, as shown in Figure 5.65:

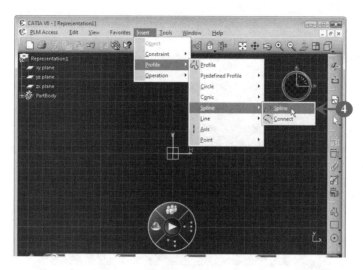

FIGURE 5.65

5. *Draw* a spline, which works as the guide curve along the profile that is to be swept (**Figure 5.66**).
6. *Click* the **Exit workbench** button on the **Workbench** toolbar to exit the Sketcher workbench, as shown in Figure 5.66:

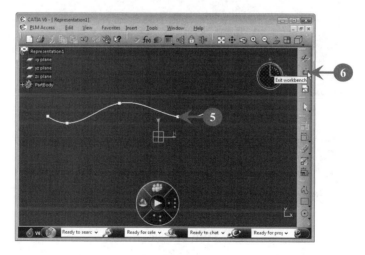

FIGURE 5.66

Figure 5.67 shows the sketch of the guide curve of the swept surface to be created in the Wireframe and Surface Design workbench:

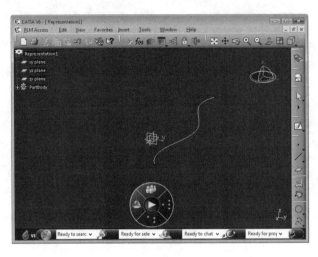

FIGURE 5.67

7. *Select* **Insert** > **Wireframe** > **Plane** from the menu bar to create a sketching plane, as shown in **Figure 5.68**:

FIGURE 5.68

The **Plane Definition** dialog box opens (**Figure 5.69**).

8. *Right-click* inside the **Reference** box and *select* the **Insert Wireframe** > **YZ-Plane** option from the context menu to specify the *yz*-plane as the reference plane for the sketching plane to be created, as shown in Figure 5.69:

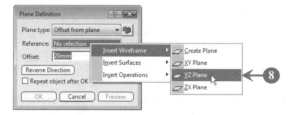

FIGURE 5.69

9. *Enter* a value representing the offset from the reference plane (*yz*-plane) in the **Offset** box (**Figure 5.70**). In our case, we continue with the default value, **20 mm**.

10. *Click* the **OK** button to close the **Plane Definition** dialog box, as shown in Figure 5.70:

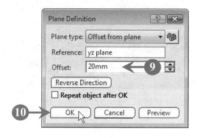

FIGURE 5.70

The sketching plane is created (**Figure 5.71**).

11. *Click* the **Sketch** button on the **Sketcher** toolbar to draw the sketch of the profile of the desired swept surface (Figure 5.71).

12. *Select* the sketching plane, as shown in Figure 5.71:

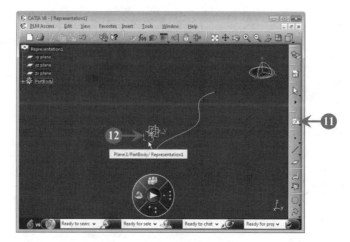

FIGURE 5.71

The Sketcher workbench is displayed with the *yz*-plane as the sketching plane (**Figure 5.72**).

13. *Select* **Insert**>**Profile**>**Circle**>**Circle** from the menu bar to draw a circle, as shown in Figure 5.72:

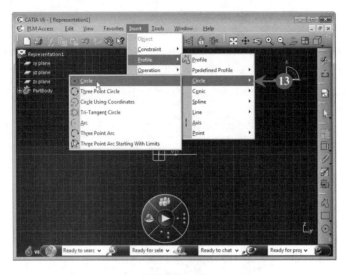

FIGURE 5.72

14. *Draw* a circle, which works as the profile to create the desired swept surface (**Figure 5.73**).
15. *Click* the **Exit workbench** button on the **Workbench** toolbar to exit the Sketcher workbench, as shown in Figure 5.73:

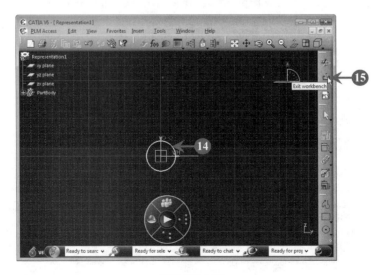

FIGURE 5.73

Figure 5.74 shows the sketch of the profile in the Wireframe and Surface Design workbench:

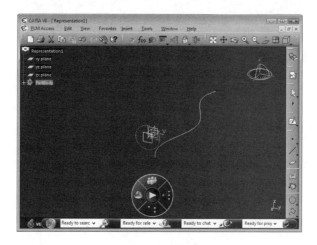

FIGURE 5.74

16. *Select* **Insert** > **Surfaces** > **Sweep** from the menu bar to create the desired swept surface, as shown in **Figure 5.75**:

FIGURE 5.75

The **Swept Surface Definition** dialog box opens (**Figure 5.76**).

17. *Select* the profile, as shown in Figure 5.76:

FIGURE 5.76

The selected profile gets added to the **Profile** box in the **Swept Surface Definition** dialog box (**Figure 5.77**).

18. *Select* the guide curve, as shown in Figure 5.77:

FIGURE 5.77

The selected guide curve is added to the **Guide curve** box in the **Swept Surface Definition** dialog box (**Figure 5.78**).

19. *Click* the **OK** button to close the **Swept Surface Definition** dialog box, as shown in Figure 5.78:

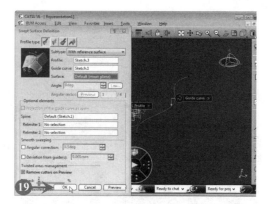

FIGURE 5.78

The resulting swept surface is shown in **Figure 5.79**:

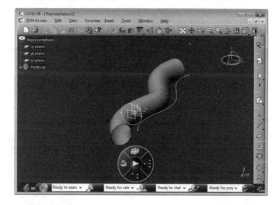

FIGURE 5.79

Creating a Fill Surface

A fill surface is a surface that is created by filling a closed profile, such as a rectangle. The closed profile works as the boundary curve for the fill surface to be created. To create a fill surface, you first need to create a boundary curve.

Perform the following steps to create a fill surface:

1. *Start* the Wireframe and Surface Design workbench.
2. *Click* the **Sketch** button on the **Sketcher** toolbar to draw the boundary curve for the desired fill surface (**Figure 5.80**).

3. *Select* the **xy-plane** option in the specification tree to invoke the Sketcher workbench with the *xy*-plane as the sketching plane, as shown in Figure 5.80:

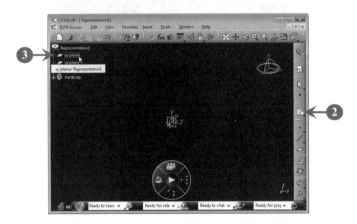

FIGURE 5.80

The Sketcher workbench is displayed with the *xy*-plane as the sketching plane (**Figure 5.81**).

4. *Select* **Insert>Profile>Predefined Profile>Rectangle** from the menu bar to draw a rectangle, as shown in Figure 5.81:

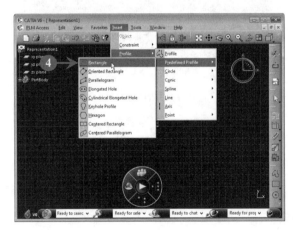

FIGURE 5.81

5. *Draw* a rectangle, which works as the boundary curve for the fill surface to be created (**Figure 5.82**).

6. *Click* the **Exit workbench** button on the **Workbench** toolbar to exit the Sketcher workbench, as shown in Figure 5.82:

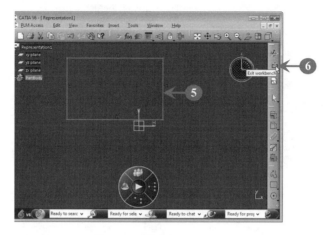

FIGURE 5.82

Figure 5.83 shows the sketch of the fill surface to be created in the Wireframe and Surface Design workbench:

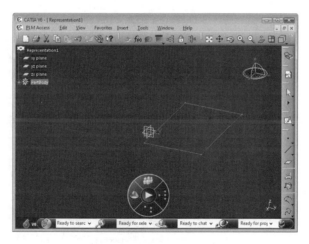

FIGURE 5.83

7. *Select* **Insert** > **Surfaces** > **Fill** from the menu bar to create the desired fill surface, as shown in **Figure 5.84**:

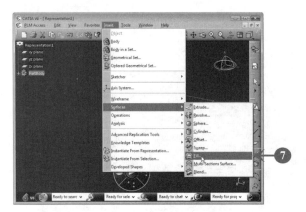

FIGURE 5.84

The **Fill Surface Definition** dialog box opens where the profile (sketch) for the desired fill surface is already added (**Figure 5.85**).

8. *Click* the **OK** button to close the **Fill Surface Definition** dialog box, as shown in Figure 5.85:

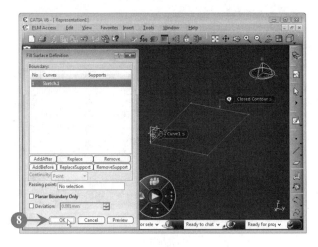

FIGURE 5.85

The resulting fill surface is shown in **Figure 5.86**:

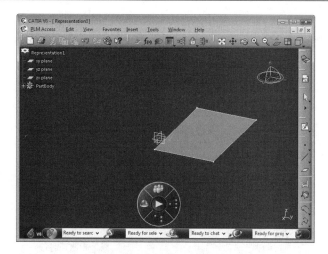

FIGURE 5.86

Creating a Multi-Sections Surface

The Wireframe and Surface Design workbench allows you to create a multi-sections surface, which is a surface created from multiple section curves using a guide curve. A multi-sections surface can be created by performing the following four broad-level steps:

1. Creating the first section curve
2. Creating the second section curve
3. Creating the guide curve
4. Creating the multi-sections surface

Let's create a multi-sections surface using these broad-level steps.

Creating the First Section Curve

Create a multi-sections curve by creating the first section curve. In addition to creating the first section curve, you also need to create two points, which can be used to create a closing point and a guide curve on the first section curve.

Perform the following steps to create the first section curve:

1. *Start* the Wireframe and Surface Design workbench.
2. *Click* the **Sketch** button on the **Sketcher** toolbar to draw the sketch of the desired multi-sections surface (**Figure 5.87**).

3. *Select* the ***xy-plane*** option in the specification tree to invoke the Sketcher workbench with the *xy*-plane as the sketching plane, as shown in Figure 5.87:

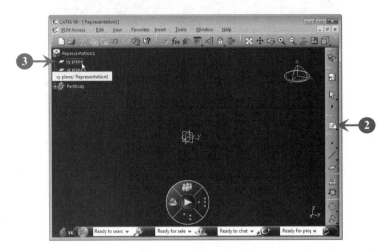

FIGURE 5.87

The Sketcher workbench gets displayed with the *xy*-plane as the sketching plane (**Figure 5.88**).

4. *Select* **Insert > Profile > Circle > Circle** from the menu bar to draw a circle, as shown in Figure 5.88:

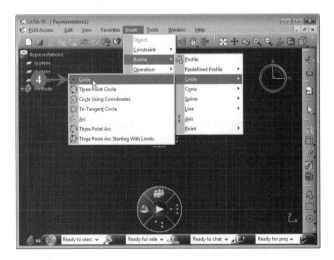

FIGURE 5.88

5. *Draw* a circle, which works as the first section curve for the multi-sections surface to be created (**Figure 5.89**).

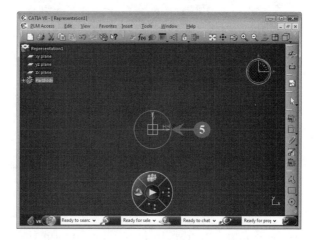

FIGURE 5.89

After creating the first section curve, you need to create two points on the first section curve that can be used to create the closing point and the guide curve.

6. *Select* **Insert** > **Profile** > **Point** > **Point** from the menu bar to create a point, as shown in **Figure 5.90**:

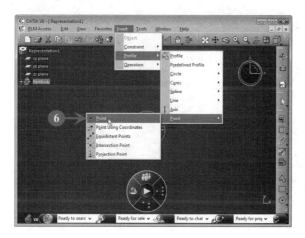

FIGURE 5.90

7. *Create* a point on the first section curve, as shown in **Figure 5.91**:

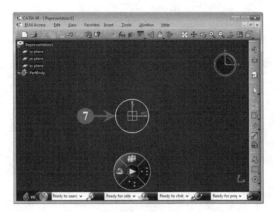

FIGURE 5.91

8. *Repeat* steps 6 and 7 to create another point on the first section curve (**Figure 5.92**).

9. *Click* the **Exit workbench** button on the Workbench toolbar to exit the Sketcher workbench, as shown in **Figure 5.92**:

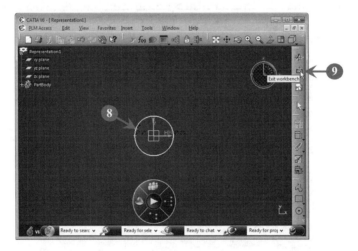

FIGURE 5.92

Figure 5.93 shows the first section curve for the multi-sections surface to be created in the Wireframe and Surface Design workbench:

FIGURE 5.93

Creating the Second Section Curve

After creating the first section curve, you need to create the second section curve. Before you create the second section curve, you need to create a sketching plane that can be used to draw the second section curve. In addition, you also need to create two points, which can be used to create a closing point and a guide curve on the second section curve.

Perform the following steps to create the second section curve:

1. *Select* **Insert>Wireframe>Plane** from the menu bar to create a sketching plane, as shown in **Figure 5.94**:

FIGURE 5.94

The **Plane Definition** dialog box opens (**Figure 5.95**).

2. *Right-click* inside the **Reference** box and *select* the **Insert Wireframe>XY-Plane** option from the context menu to specify the *xy*-plane as the reference plane for the sketching plane to be created, as shown in Figure 5.95:

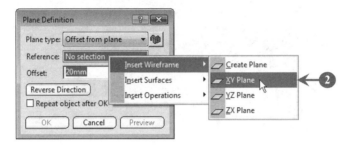

FIGURE 5.95

3. *Enter* a value representing the offset from the reference plane (*xy*-plane) in the **Offset** box (**Figure 5.96**). In our case, we have entered **50 mm**.
4. *Click* the **OK** button to close the **Plane Definition** dialog box, as shown in Figure 5.96:

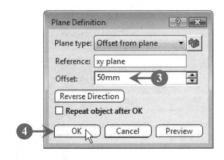

FIGURE 5.96

The sketching plane is created (**Figure 5.97**).

5. *Click* the **Sketch** button on the **Sketcher** toolbar to draw the sketch of the profile of the desired multi-sections surface (Figure 5.97).
6. *Select* the sketching plane, as shown in Figure 5.97:

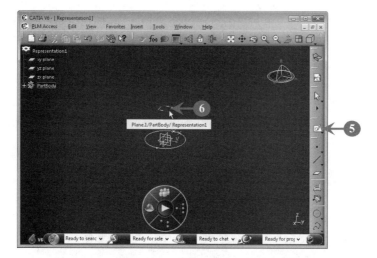

FIGURE 5.97

The Sketcher workbench is displayed with the *xy*-plane as the sketching plane (**Figure 5.98**).

7. *Select* **Insert > Profile > Circle > Circle** from the menu bar to draw a circle, as shown in Figure 5.98:

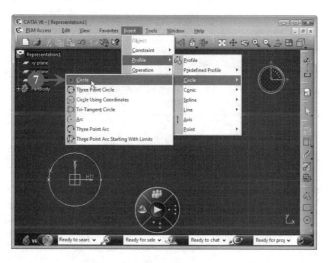

FIGURE 5.98

8. *Draw* a circle, which works as the second section curve for the multi-sections surface to be created (**Figure 5.99**).
9. *Create* two points on the second section curve (as done for the first section curve) that can be used to create the closing point and the guide curve on the second section curve (Figure 5.99).

10. *Click* the **Exit workbench** button on the **Workbench** toolbar to exit the Sketcher workbench, as shown in Figure 5.99:

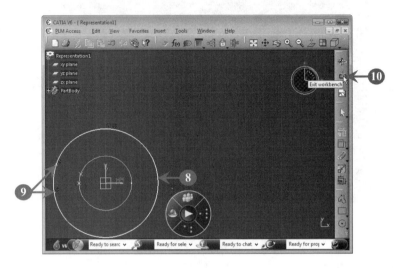

FIGURE 5.99

Figure 5.100 shows the second section curve for the multi-sections surface to be created in the Wireframe and Surface Design workbench:

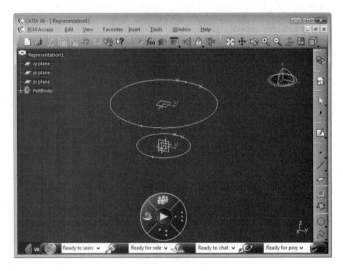

FIGURE 5.100

Creating the Guide Curve

After creating the two section curves, you need to create the guide curve that can be used to create the multi-sections surface from the two section curves. You can create the guide curve by creating a line, using the two points (one from each of the two section curves) as the starting and ending points for the line.

Perform the following steps to create the guide curve:

1. *Select* **Insert**>**Wireframe**>**Line** from the menu bar to create a line, which can be used as the guide curve to create the multi-sections surface, as shown in **Figure 5.101**:

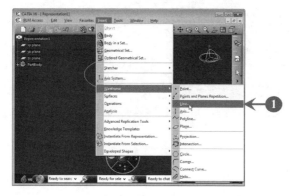

FIGURE 5.101

The **Line Definition** dialog box opens (**Figure 5.102**).

2. *Select* a point on the first section curve, as shown in Figure 5.102:

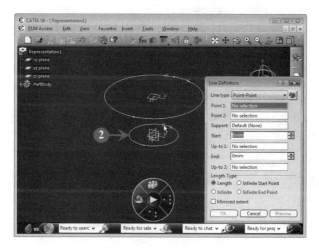

FIGURE 5.102

The selected point is added to the **Point 1** box in the **Line Definition** dialog box (**Figure 5.103**).

3. *Select* a point on the second section curve, as shown in Figure 5.103:

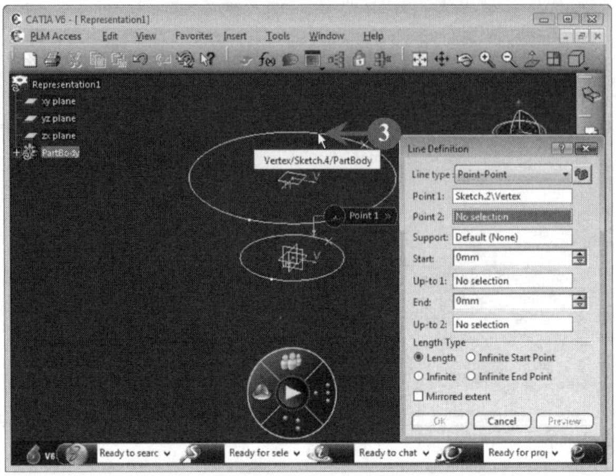

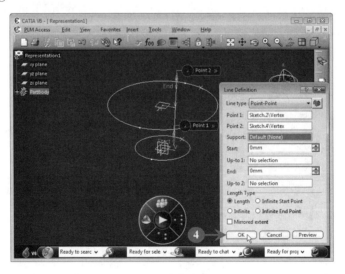

FIGURE 5.103

The selected point is added to the **Point 2** box in the **Line Definition** dialog box (**Figure 5.104**).

4. *Click* the **OK** button to close the **Line Definition** dialog box, as shown in Figure 5.104:

FIGURE 5.104

A line joining the two selected points on the two section curves is created, as shown in **Figure 5.105**:

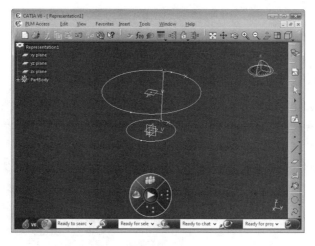

FIGURE 5.105

You have learned to create the section curves and the guide curve. We next learn how to create the multi-sections surface.

Creating the Multi-Sections Surface

Once you have created the two section curves and the guide curve, you can create the multi-sections surface. For this purpose, you first need to select the two section curves, create closing points on these curves, and then select the guide curve.

Perform the following steps to create the multi-sections surface:

1. *Select* **Insert > Surfaces > Multi-Sections Surface** from the menu bar to create the desired multi-sections surface, as shown in **Figure 5.106**:

FIGURE 5.106

The **Multi-Sections Surface Definition** dialog box opens (**Figure 5.107**).

2. *Select* the first section curve, as shown in Figure 5.107:

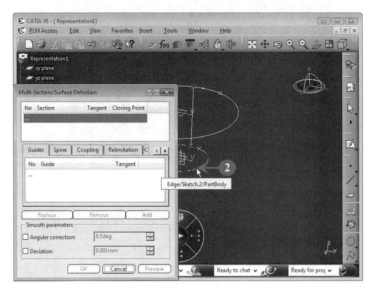

FIGURE 5.107

The first section curve is added to the **Multi-Sections Surface Definition** dialog box, and a default closing point is also created on the first section curve (**Figure 5.108**).

3. *Right-click* the text associated with the default closing point and *select* the **Replace** option from the context menu, as shown in Figure 5.108:

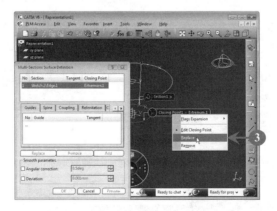

FIGURE 5.108

4. *Select* another point on the first section curve, as shown in **Figure 5.109**:

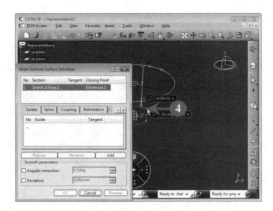

FIGURE 5.109

The selected point becomes the closing point on the first section curve (**Figure 5.110**).

5. *Click* the **Add** button to select the second section curve, as shown in Figure 5.110:

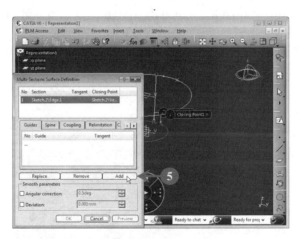

FIGURE 5.110

6. *Select* the second section curve, as shown in **Figure 5.111**:

FIGURE 5.111

The second section curve is added to the **Multi-Sections Surface Definition** dialog box, and a default closing point is also created on the second section curve (**Figure 5.112**).

7. *Repeat* steps 3 and 4 to replace the default closing point on the second section curve with the second point on the second section curve (Figure 5.112).
8. *Click* inside the pane of the **Guides** tab to select the guide curve, as shown in Figure 5.112:

FIGURE 5.112

The first row of the pane of the **Guides** tab is selected (Figure 5.113).

9. *Select* the guide curve; that is, the line joining the two section curves, as shown in **Figure 5.113**:

FIGURE 5.113

The guide curve is added to the pane of the **Guides** tab (**Figure 5.114**).

10. *Click* the **OK** button to close the **Multi-Sections Surface Definition** dialog box, as shown in Figure 5.114:

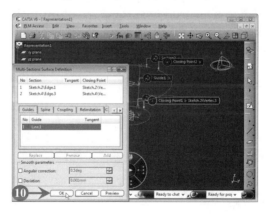

FIGURE 5.114

The resulting multi-sections surface is shown in **Figure 5.115**:

FIGURE 5.115

We next summarize the main topics covered in this chapter.

SUMMARY

In this chapter, you have learned how to create:

- Wireframe elements such as a point, line, plane, and circle
- Surfaces such as an extruded surface, revolved surface, swept surface, and multi-sections surface

Chapter 6

GENERATIVE SHEET METAL DESIGN WORKBENCH

The Generative Sheet Metal Design workbench is a workbench of CATIA V6 that allows you to design sheet metal components. A sheet metal component is a component having thickness in the range of 0.142 to 1681 inches. The first step in designing a sheet metal component is creating sections of the sheet metal component. These sections are known as sheet metal walls. Once you have created sheet metal walls for your sheet metal component, you can give the desired shape to the sheet metal component by performing many types of operations, such as bending and cutting on the sheet metal walls.

In this chapter, you learn how to create different types of sheet metal walls. You also learn how to create bends in sheet metal walls. Finally, you learn how to cut sheet metal walls. Let's begin our discussion with creating sheet metal walls.

6.1 CREATING SHEET METAL WALLS

A sheet metal wall can be of many types, such as a base wall, a wall on edge, an extrusion wall, and a swept wall. To create a sheet metal component, first create a base wall and then you can create other walls with respect to the base wall. When you create sheet metal walls, you need to set different parameters, known as sheet metal parameters, for your sheet metal walls. These parameters include sheet metal thickness and default bend radius. Sheet metal thickness is the depth of the sheet metal wall, and default bend radius is the default radius with which a bend is created on a sheet metal wall.

In this section, you learn how to create the following four types of sheet metal walls:

- Base wall
- Wall on edge
- Extrusion wall
- Swept wall

We begin by learning how to create a base wall.

Creating a Base Wall

A base wall is a section of a sheet metal component that is created before all other sections of the sheet metal component. To create a base wall, first you need to set sheet metal parameters, then draw the sketch of the base wall in the Sketcher workbench, and finally convert the sketch into the base wall in the Generative Sheet Metal Design workbench.

Perform the following steps to create a base wall:

1. *Open* CATIA V6.
2. *Select* **Start > Mechanical Design > Generative Sheet Metal Design** on the CATIA V6 user interface to start the Generative Sheet Metal Design workbench, as shown in **Figure 6.1**:

FIGURE 6.1

The **3D Shape/Representation DS** dialog box opens (**Figure 6.2**).

3. *Enter* a name for the representation in the **Representation Name** text box (Figure 6.2). In our case, we continue with the default name, **Representation1**.
4. *Click* the **Finish** button to close the **3D Shape/Representation DS** dialog box, as shown in Figure 6.2:

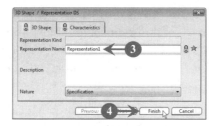

FIGURE 6.2

A new representation, **Representation1**, is created in the Generative Sheet Metal Design workbench, as shown in **Figure 6.3**:

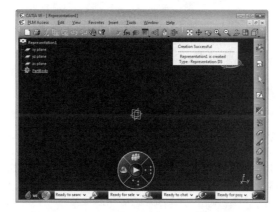

FIGURE 6.3

5. *Select* **Insert > Sheet Metal Parameters** from the menu bar to set the sheet metal parameters, as shown in **Figure 6.4**:

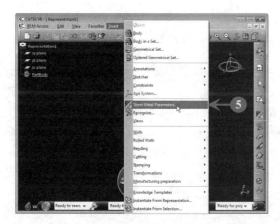

FIGURE 6.4

The **Sheet Metal Parameters Definition** dialog box opens (**Figure 6.5**). This dialog box allows you to set different sheet metal parameters, such as sheet metal thickness and default bend radius, for the sheet metal walls. You can either use the default values for these parameters or specify new values. In our case, we are using the default values for the sheet metal parameters.

6.   *Click* the **OK** button to close the **Sheet Metal Parameters Definition** dialog box, as shown in Figure 6.5:

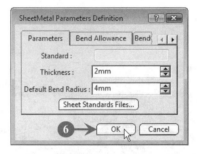

FIGURE 6.5

A node with the name **Sheet Metal Parameters.1** is added to the specification tree (**Figure 6.6**). Now, you need to draw the sketch of the base wall using the Sketcher workbench. You can invoke the Sketcher workbench by first clicking the **Sketch** button on the **Sketcher** toolbar and then selecting a sketching plane in the specification tree.

7.   *Click* the **Sketch** button on the **Sketcher** toolbar (Figure 6.6).

8.   *Select* the ***xy*-plane** option from the specification tree, as shown in Figure 6.6:

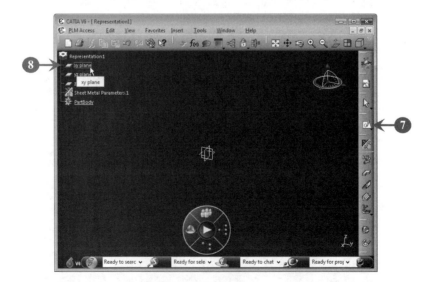

FIGURE 6.6

The Sketcher workbench is displayed with *xy*-plane as the sketching plane (**Figure 6.7**).

9. *Draw* a sketch in the Sketcher workbench (Figure 6.7). In our case, we have drawn a rectangle.

10. *Click* the **Exit workbench** button on the **Workbench** toolbar to exit the Sketcher workbench, as shown in Figure 6.7:

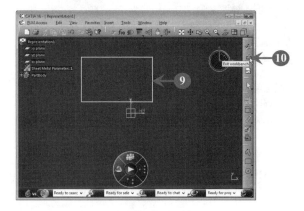

FIGURE 6.7

The Sketcher workbench closes and the Generative Sheet Metal Design workbench is displayed (**Figure 6.8**).

11. *Select* the sketch, as shown in Figure 6.8:

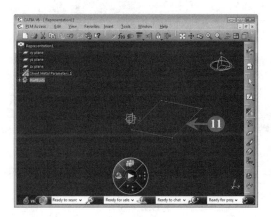

FIGURE 6.8

12. *Select* **Insert**>**Walls**>**Wall** from the menu bar to create a base wall, as shown in **Figure 6.9**:

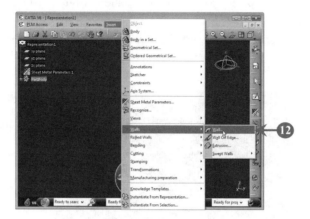

FIGURE 6.9

The **Wall Definition** dialog box opens (**Figure 6.10**). Notice that the sketch is added to the **Profile** box of the **Wall Definition** dialog box.

13. *Click* the **OK** button to close the **Wall Definition** dialog box, as shown in Figure 6.10:

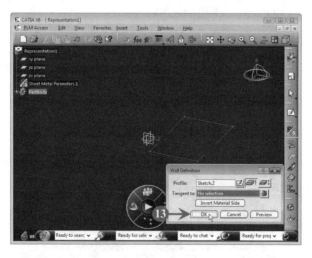

FIGURE 6.10

The base wall is created from the sketch, as shown in **Figure 6.11**:

FIGURE 6.11

After creating the base wall, you can create other types of walls, such as a wall on edge, an extrusion wall, and a swept wall. We first learn how to create a wall on edge.

Creating a Wall on Edge

After creating a base wall, you can create a wall, called a wall on edge, on an edge of the base wall. A wall on edge uses the same values for the sheet metal parameters that were defined for the base wall.

Perform the following steps to create a wall on edge:

1. *Start* the Generative Sheet Metal Design workbench.
2. *Create* a base wall (**Figure 6.12**).
3. *Select* the edge of the base wall on which you want to create a wall, as shown in Figure 6.12:

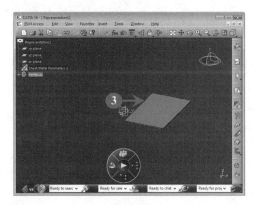

FIGURE 6.12

4. *Select* **Insert** > **Walls** > **Wall On Edge** from the menu bar to create a wall
    on an edge of the base wall, as shown in **Figure 6.13**:

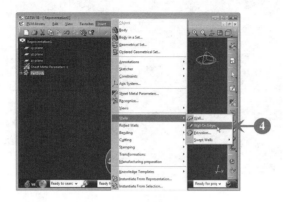

FIGURE 6.13

The **Wall On Edge Definition** dialog box opens (**Figure 6.14**).

5. *Set* options, such as height and angle of inclination, for the wall to be created
    in the **Wall On Edge Definition** dialog box (Figure 6.14). In our case, we
    have set the height of the wall as **100 mm**.

6. *Click* the **OK** button to close the **Wall On Edge Definition** dialog box, as
    shown in Figure 6.14:

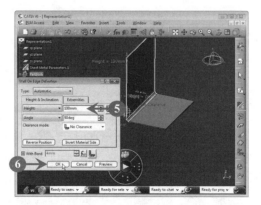

FIGURE 6.14

A wall is created on the selected edge of the base wall, as shown in **Figure 6.15**:

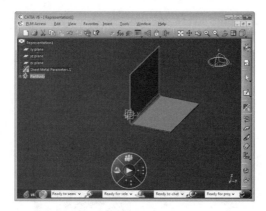

FIGURE 6.15

We next learn how to create an extrusion wall.

Creating an Extrusion Wall

An extrusion wall is a wall that is created by extruding an open sketch, such as a line, drawn on an existing wall. A wall created by extrusion does not have a bend. You can later create a bend at the intersection of the base wall and the extrusion wall. You learn how to create bends in the section, *Bending Sheet Metal Walls*, later in this chapter.

Perform the following steps to create an extrusion wall:

1. *Start* the Generative Sheet Metal Design workbench.
2. *Create* a base wall (**Figure 6.16**).

Now, you need to draw the sketch of the extrusion wall using the Sketcher workbench.

3. *Click* the **Sketch** button on the **Sketcher** toolbar (Figure 6.16).
4. *Select* the **xy-plane** option from the specification tree, as shown in Figure 6.16:

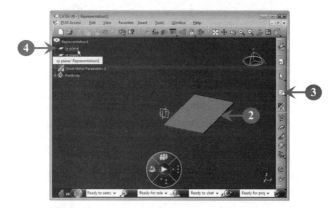

FIGURE 6.16

The Sketcher workbench is displayed with xy-plane as the sketching plane (**Figure 6.17**).

5. *Draw* a sketch on the base wall (Figure 6.17). In our case, we have drawn a line.

6. *Click* the **Exit workbench** button on the **Workbench** toolbar to exit the Sketcher workbench, as shown in Figure 6.17:

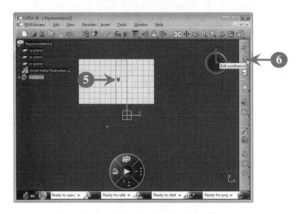

FIGURE 6.17

The Sketcher workbench closes and the Generative Sheet Metal Design workbench is displayed (**Figure 6.18**).

7. *Select* the sketch, as shown in Figure 6.18:

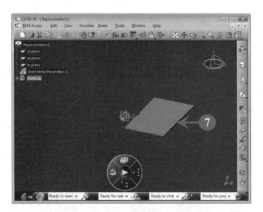

FIGURE 6.18

8. *Select* **Insert > Walls > Extrusion** from the menu bar to create an extrusion wall, as shown in **Figure 6.19**:

FIGURE 6.19

The **Extrusion Definition** dialog box opens (**Figure 6.20**).

9. *Set* options, such as Limit 1 and Limit 2 dimensions, for the extrusion wall to be created in the **Extrusion Definition** dialog box (Figure 6.20). In our case, we have set the value of the **Limit 1 dimension** option as **50 mm**.

10. *Click* the **Invert direction** button to reverse the direction of extrusion, if required, as shown in Figure 6.20:

FIGURE 6.20

11. *Click* the **OK** button to close the **Extrusion Definition** dialog box, as shown in **Figure 6.21**:

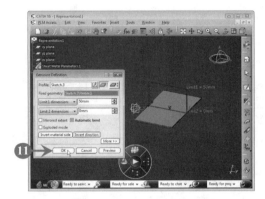

FIGURE 6.21

If the extrusion operation does not result in a closed sheet metal component, a message box showing a warning message may appear (**Figure 6.22**).

12. *Click* the **Close** button to close the message box, as shown in Figure 6.22:

FIGURE 6.22

The sketch is extruded to create an extrusion wall, as shown in **Figure 6.23**:

FIGURE 6.23

We next learn how to create a swept wall.

Creating a Swept Wall

A swept wall is a wall that is created by sweeping a sheet metal wall along one of its edges. In the process of sweeping a wall, the wall is extended in such a manner that a bend is created on its edge. A swept wall can be of many types, such as flange, hem, and tear drop.

In this section, you learn about the following three types of swept walls:

- Flange
- Hem
- Tear drop

Let's discuss each of these, one by one.

Creating a Flange

A flange is a swept wall that is created by sweeping a sheet metal wall along one of its edges with an angle greater than or equal to 0 degrees and less than 180 degrees.

Perform the following steps to create a flange on an edge of a sheet metal wall:

1. *Start* the Generative Sheet Metal Design workbench.
2. *Create* a base wall (**Figure 6.24**).
3. *Select* the edge of the base wall on which you want to create a flange, as shown in Figure 6.24:

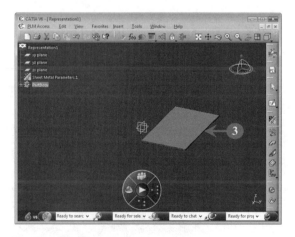

FIGURE 6.24

4. *Select* **Insert > Walls > Swept Walls > Flange** from the menu bar to create a flange, as shown in **Figure 6.25**:

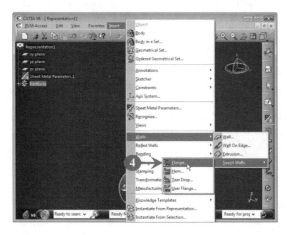

FIGURE 6.25

The **Flange Definition** dialog box opens (**Figure 6.26**). This dialog box allows you to set different options for the flange, such as the length of the flange, angle of the flange with the base wall, and radius for the bend that will be created at the intersection of the base wall and the flange. You can either use the default values for these options or specify new values. In our case, we are using the default values for flange options.

5. *Click* the **OK** button to close the **Flange Definition** dialog box, as shown in Figure 6.26:

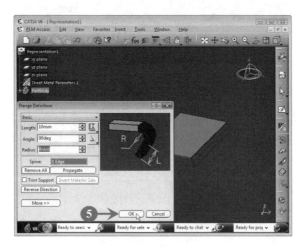

FIGURE 6.26

A flange is created on the selected edge of the base wall, as shown in **Figure 6.27**:

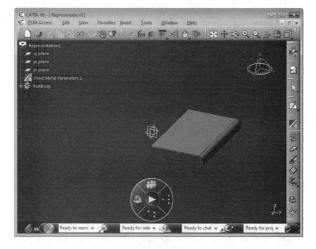

FIGURE 6.27

In the same way, you can also create a flange on another edge of the base wall, as shown in **Figure 6.28**:

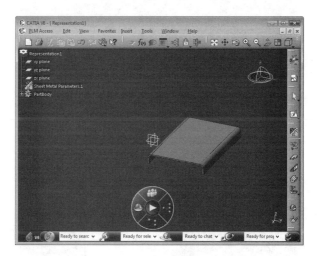

FIGURE 6.28

We next learn how to create another type of swept wall, a hem.

Creating a Hem

A hem is a swept wall that is created by sweeping a sheet metal wall along one of its edges with an angle equal to 0 degrees; it means that a hem is parallel to the existing wall. Hems are generally created on the sharp edges of a sheet metal component to reduce the sharpness of the edges. This makes handling sheet metal components easier.

Perform the following steps to create a hem on an edge of a sheet metal wall:

1. *Start* the Generative Sheet Metal Design workbench.
2. *Create* a base wall (**Figure 6.29**).
3. *Select* the edge of the base wall on which you want to create a hem, as shown in Figure 6.29:

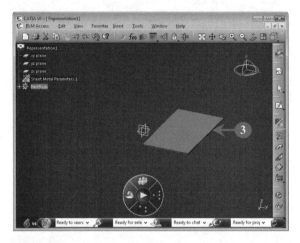

FIGURE 6.29

4. *Select* **Insert > Walls > Swept Walls > Hem** from the menu bar to create a hem, as shown in **Figure 6.30**:

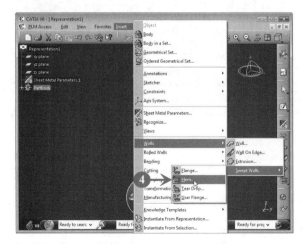

FIGURE 6.30

The **Hem Definition** dialog box opens (**Figure 6.31**). This dialog box allows you to set different options for the hem, such as the length of the hem and radius for the bend that will be created at the intersection of the base wall and the hem. You can either use the default values for these options or specify new values. In our case, we are using the default values for hem options.

5. *Click* the **OK** button to close the **Hem Definition** dialog box, as shown in Figure 6.31:

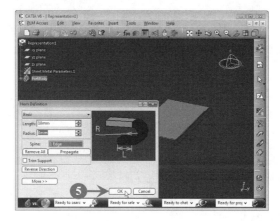

FIGURE 6.31

A hem is created on the selected edge of the base wall, as shown in **Figure 6.32**:

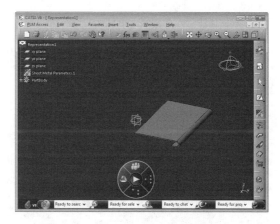

FIGURE 6.32

In the same way, you can also create a hem on another edge of the base wall, as shown in **Figure 6.33**:

FIGURE 6.33

We next learn how to create a tear drop swept wall.

Creating a Tear Drop

A tear drop is similar to a hem but instead of being parallel to the wall on which it is created, it touches the wall.

Perform the following steps to create a tear drop on an edge of a sheet metal wall:

1. *Start* the Generative Sheet Metal Design workbench.
2. *Create* a base wall (**Figure 6.34**).
3. *Select* the edge of the base wall on which you want to create a tear drop, as shown in Figure 6.34:

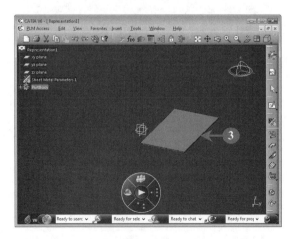

FIGURE 6.34

4. *Select* **Insert > Walls > Swept Walls > Tear Drop** from the menu bar to create a tear drop, as shown in **Figure 6.35**:

FIGURE 6.35

The **Tear Drop Definition** dialog box opens (**Figure 6.36**). This dialog box allows you to set different options for the tear drop, such as the length of the tear drop and radius for the bend that will be created at the intersection of the base wall and the tear drop. You can either use the default values for these options or specify new values. In our case, we are using the default values for tear drop options.

5. *Click* the **OK** button to close the **Tear Drop Definition** dialog box, as shown in Figure 6.36:

FIGURE 6.36

A tear drop is created on the selected edge of the base wall, as shown in **Figure 6.37**:

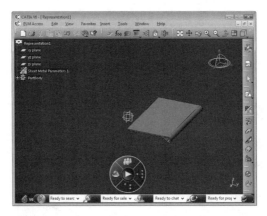

FIGURE 6.37

In the same way, you can also create a tear drop on another edge of the base wall, as shown in **Figure 6.38**:

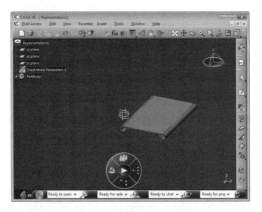

FIGURE 6.38

After learning how to create sheet metal walls, we next learn how to create bends in sheet metal walls.

6.2 BENDING SHEET METAL WALLS

Bending sheet metal walls implies creating a bend or bent face at the intersection of two walls. Bends can be of two types: bends having a fixed radius and bends having a variable radius. You can either create a bend on the intersection of two walls or create a bend on a wall by first drawing a sketch on the wall. Other operations related to bending are unfolding and folding bends.

In this section, you learn to perform the following five operations related to bending:

- Creating a fixed-radius bend
- Creating a variable-radius bend
- Creating a bend from a sketch
- Unfolding a bend
- Folding a bend

Let's discuss each of these, one by one.

Creating a Fixed-Radius Bend

A fixed-radius bend is a bend that has the same radius at both ends and between the ends.

Perform the following steps to create a fixed radius bend:

1. *Start* the Generative Sheet Metal Design workbench.
2. *Create* a base wall, as shown in **Figure 6.39**:

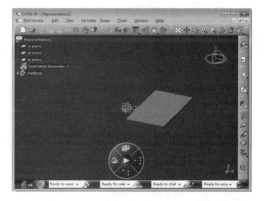

FIGURE 6.39

3. *Create* a wall by extruding one of the edges of the base wall, as shown in **Figure 6.40**:

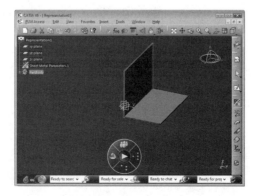

FIGURE 6.40

4. *Select* **Insert**>**Bending**>**Bend** from the menu bar to create a bend, as shown in **Figure 6.41**:

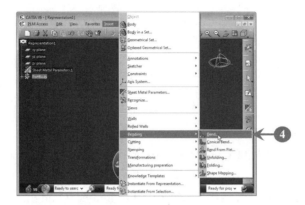

FIGURE 6.41

The **Bend Definition** dialog box opens (**Figure 6.42**).

5. *Select* the base wall, as shown in Figure 6.42:

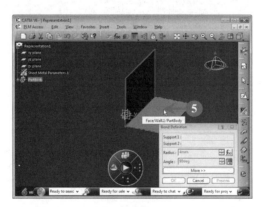

FIGURE 6.42

The base wall is added to the **Bend Definition** dialog box (**Figure 6.43**).

6. *Select* another wall, as shown in Figure 6.43:

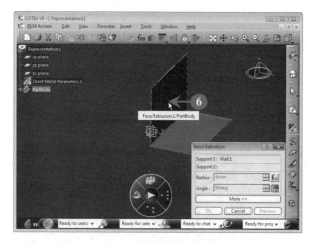

FIGURE 6.43

The selected wall is added to the **Bend Definition** dialog box (**Figure 6.44**).

7. *Click* the **OK** button to close the **Bend Definition** dialog box, as shown in Figure 6.44:

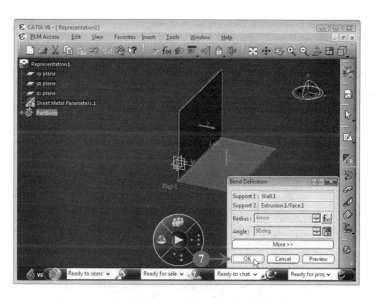

FIGURE 6.44

A fixed-radius bend is created between the two walls, as shown in **Figure 6.45**:

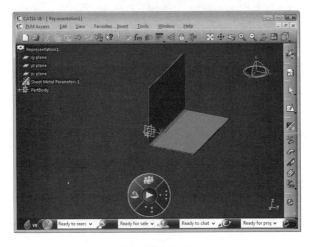

FIGURE 6.45

We next learn how to create a variable-radius bend.

Creating a Variable-Radius Bend

You can also create bends with variable radius at the intersection of two walls. The radius of a variable-radius bend varies from one end to another end of the bent face. Bends with variable radius are also known as conical bends.

Perform the following steps to create a variable-radius bend:

1. *Start* the Generative Sheet Metal Design workbench.
2. *Create* a base wall and then create a wall by extruding one of the edges of the base wall, as shown in **Figure 6.46**:

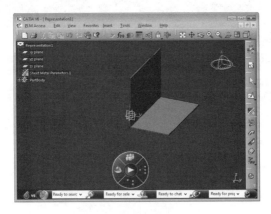

FIGURE 6.46

3. *Select* **Insert**>**Bending**>**Conical Bend** from the menu bar to create a conical bend, as shown in **Figure 6.47**:

FIGURE 6.47

The **Bend Definition** dialog box opens (**Figure 6.48**).

4. *Select* the base wall, as shown in Figure 6.48:

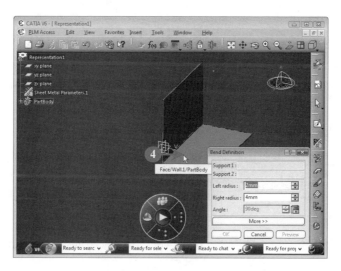

FIGURE 6.48

The base wall is added to the **Bend Definition** dialog box (**Figure 6.49**).

5. *Select* another wall, as shown in Figure 6.49:

FIGURE 6.49

The selected wall is added to the **Bend Definition** dialog box (**Figure 6.50**).

6. *Set* options, such as left radius and right radius, for the bend to be created in the **Bend Definition** dialog box (Figure 6.50). In our case, we have set the left radius for the bend as **8 mm**.

7. *Click* the **OK** button to close the **Bend Definition** dialog box, as shown in Figure 6.50:

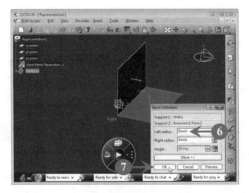

FIGURE 6.50

A variable-radius bend is created between the two walls, as shown in **Figure 6.51**:

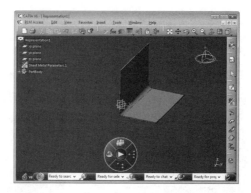

FIGURE 6.51

We next learn how to create a bend from a sketch.

Creating a Bend from a Sketch

It is not necessary to have two walls before creating a bend; you can create a bend with only a single wall. If you want to create a bend on a sheet metal wall, you first need to draw a sketch on the wall in the Sketcher workbench and then use this sketch to create a bend in the Generative Sheet Metal Design workbench.

Perform the following steps to create a bend from a sketch:

1. *Start* the Generative Sheet Metal Design workbench.
2. *Create* a base wall and then *draw* a sketch on the base wall using the Sketcher workbench. In our case, we have drawn a line on the base wall, as shown in **Figure 6.52**:

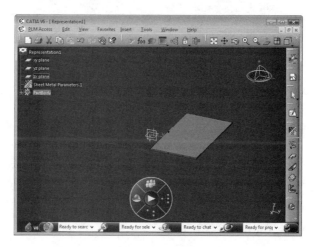

FIGURE 6.52

3. *Select* **Insert>Bending>Bend From Flat** from the menu bar to create a bend from the sketch, as shown in **Figure 6.53**:

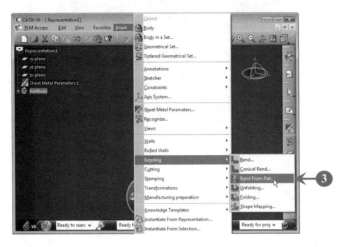

FIGURE 6.53

The **Bend From Flat Definition** dialog box opens (**Figure 6.54**).

4. *Reverse* the bending direction by clicking the blue arrow, if required, as shown in Figure 6.54:

FIGURE 6.54

5. *Click* the **OK** button to close the **Bend From Flat Definition** dialog box, as shown in **Figure 6.55**:

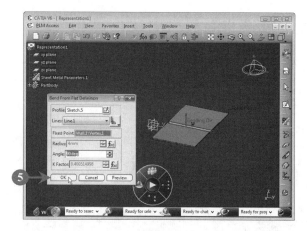

FIGURE 6.55

A bend is created from the sketch, as shown in **Figure 6.56**:

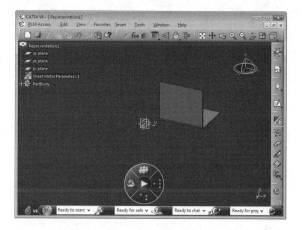

FIGURE 6.56

After learning how to create bends, we next learn how to unfold and fold bends.

Unfolding a Bend

After creating a bend between two walls, you may sometimes need to unfold the bent face. Unfolding a bend is generally needed in situations where you want to perform operations that cannot be performed on a bent face, such as creating a cutout and hole across the bent face of a wall. To perform such operations, you need to unfold the bent face.

Perform the following steps to unfold a bend:

1. *Start* the Generative Sheet Metal Design workbench.

2. *Create* a base wall and then *draw* a sketch on the base wall using the Sketcher workbench. In our case, we have drawn a line on the base wall, as shown in **Figure 6.57**:

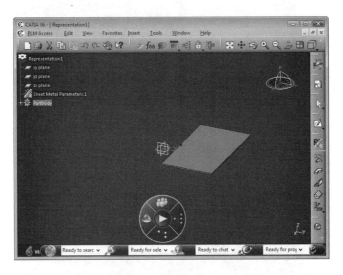

FIGURE 6.57

3. *Create* a bend from the sketch, as shown in **Figure 6.58**:

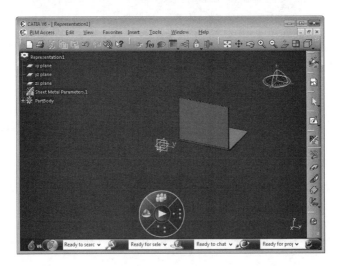

FIGURE 6.58

4. *Select* **Insert** > **Bending** > **Unfolding** from the menu bar to unfold a bend, as shown in **Figure 6.59**:

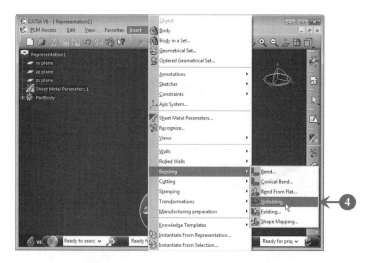

FIGURE 6.59

The **Unfolding Definition** dialog box opens (**Figure 6.60**).

5. *Select* the base wall, as shown in Figure 6.60:

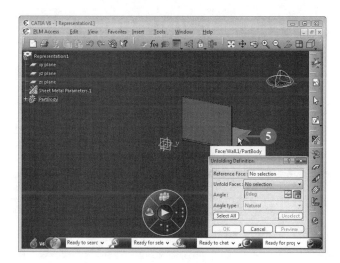

FIGURE 6.60

The base wall is added to the **Unfolding Definition** dialog box (**Figure 6.61**).

6. *Select* the bent face, as shown in Figure 6.61:

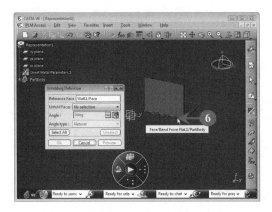

FIGURE 6.61

The bent face is added to the **Unfolding Definition** dialog box (**Figure 6.62**).

7. *Click* the **OK** button to close the **Unfolding Definition** dialog box, as shown in Figure 6.62:

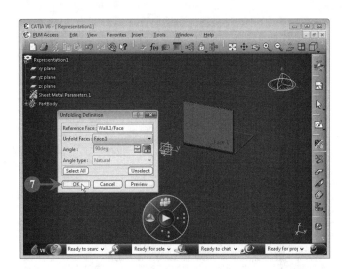

FIGURE 6.62

The bend is unfolded, as shown in **Figure 6.63**:

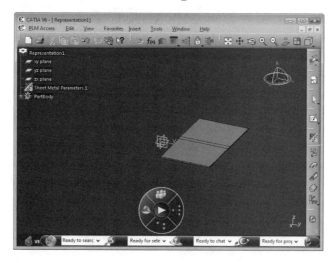

FIGURE 6.63

We next learn how to fold bends.

Folding a Bend

As mentioned earlier, you need to unfold the bent face of a wall before you perform certain operations, such as creating a cutout or hole on it. Once you have performed such operations, you need to fold the unfolded face of the wall.

Perform the following steps to fold a bend:

1. *Start* the Generative Sheet Metal Design workbench.

2. *Create* a base wall, as shown in **Figure 6.64**:

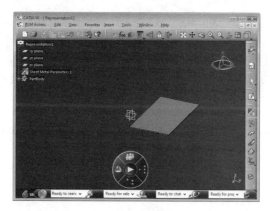

FIGURE 6.64

3. *Create* a bend on the base wall by selecting **Insert** > **Walls** > **Wall On Edge** from the menu bar, as shown in **Figure 6.65**:

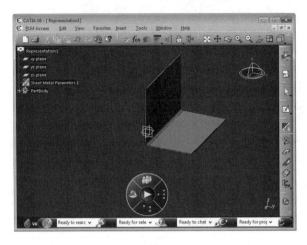

FIGURE 6.65

4. *Unfold* the bend by selecting **Insert** > **Bending** > **Unfolding** from the menu bar, as shown in **Figure 6.66**:

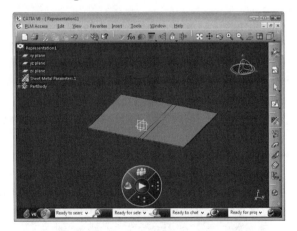

FIGURE 6.66

5. *Select* **Insert** > **Bending** > **Folding** from the menu bar to fold the bend again, as shown in **Figure 6.67**:

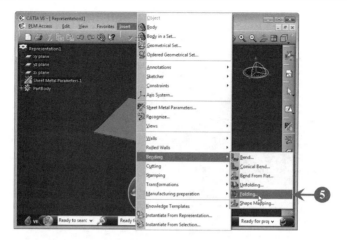

FIGURE 6.67

The **Folding Definition** dialog box opens (**Figure 6.68**).

6. *Select* the base wall, as shown in Figure 6.68:

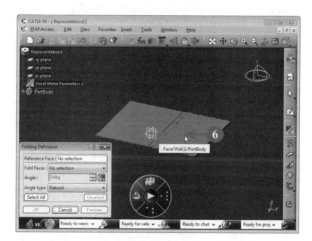

FIGURE 6.68

The base wall is added to the **Folding Definition** dialog box (**Figure 6.69**).

7. *Select* the bending face, as shown in Figure 6.69:

FIGURE 6.69

The bending face is added to the **Folding Definition** dialog box (**Figure 6.70**).

8. *Click* the **OK** button to close the **Folding Definition** dialog box, as shown in Figure 6.70:

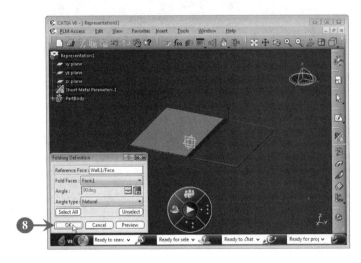

FIGURE 6.70

The bend is folded again, as shown in **Figure 6.71**:

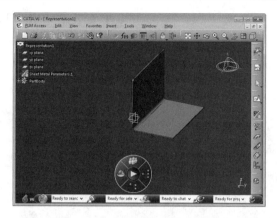

FIGURE 6.71

Similar to bending, another important operation that can be performed on a sheet metal wall is cutting, which is discussed next.

6.3 CUTTING SHEET METAL WALLS

Cutting a sheet metal wall implies removing a portion from the sheet metal wall. CATIA V6 provides options to cut a sheet metal wall in different ways. For example, it allows you to create a cutout of a specific geometric shape, a circular cutout, a hole, and corners.

In this section, you learn to perform the following four cutting operations on sheet metal walls:

- Creating a cutout of a specified shape
- Creating a circular cutout
- Creating a hole
- Creating corners

Let's discuss each of these, one by one.

Creating a Cutout of a Specified Shape

In CATIA V6, you can create a cutout of a desired shape on a sheet metal wall. First, draw the sketch of the cutout on the wall in the Sketcher workbench, and then you can create the cutout in the Generative Sheet Metal workbench. In this way, you can create different types of cutouts, such as rectangular, triangular, circular, and elliptical cutouts.

Perform the following steps to create a cutout of a specified shape:

1. *Start* the Generative Sheet Metal Design workbench.
2. *Create* a base wall, as shown in **Figure 6.72**:

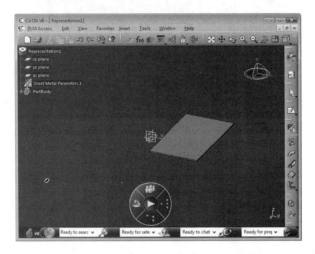

FIGURE 6.72

3. *Draw* a sketch on the base wall using the Sketcher workbench. In our case, we have drawn a rectangle, as shown in **Figure 6.73**:

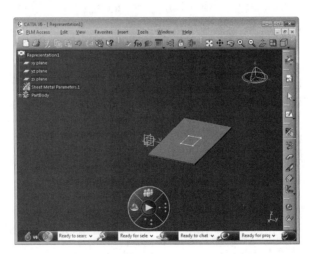

FIGURE 6.73

4. *Select* **Insert > Cutting > Cut Out** from the menu bar to create a cutout, as shown in **Figure 6.74**:

FIGURE 6.74

The **Cutout Definition** dialog box opens (**Figure 6.75**).

5. *Select* the sketch drawn on the base wall, as shown in Figure 6.75:

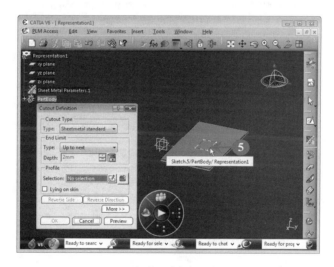

FIGURE 6.75

The sketch is added to the **Cutout Definition** dialog box (**Figure 6.76**).

6. *Click* the **OK** button to close the **Cutout Definition** dialog box, as shown in Figure 6.76:

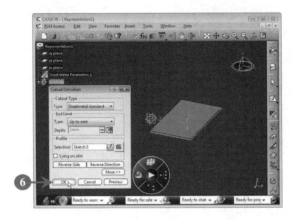

FIGURE 6.76

A rectangular cutout is created on the base wall, as shown in **Figure 6.77**:

FIGURE 6.77

We next learn how to create a circular cutout.

Creating a Circular Cutout

CATIA V6 allows you to create a circular cutout on a sheet metal wall without drawing the sketch of the cutout in the Sketcher workbench. You can specify the shape of the cutout while creating the cutout in the Generative Sheet Metal Design workbench.

Perform the following steps to create a circular cutout:

1. *Start* the Generative Sheet Metal Design workbench.
2. *Create* a base wall, as shown in **Figure 6.78**:

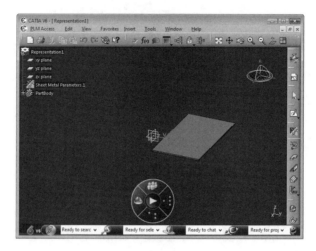

FIGURE 6.78

3. *Select* **Insert>Cutting>Circular Cutout** from the menu bar to create a circular cutout, as shown in **Figure 6.79**:

FIGURE 6.79

The **Circular Cutout Definition** dialog box opens (**Figure 6.80**).

4. *Select* a point on the base wall where you want to create a circular cutout, as shown in Figure 6.80:

FIGURE 6.80

The selected point is added to the **Circular Cutout Definition** dialog box (**Figure 6.81**).

5. *Enter* a value representing the diameter of the circular cutout in the **Diameter** box in the **Diameter** group (Figure 6.81). In our case, we have entered **20 mm**.

6. *Click* the **OK** button to close the **Circular Cutout Definition** dialog box, as shown in Figure 6.81:

FIGURE 6.81

The circular cutout is created on the base wall, as shown in **Figure 6.82**:

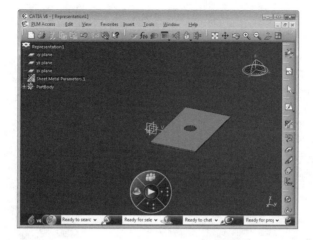

FIGURE 6.82

We next learn how to create a hole on a sheet metal wall.

Creating a Hole

CATIA V6 allows you to create a hole on a sheet metal wall. A hole can be of many types, such as a simple hole, tapered hole, counterbored hole, countersunk hole, and counterdrilled hole. A simple hole is equivalent to a circular cutout.

Perform the following steps to create a hole:

1. *Start* the Generative Sheet Metal Design workbench.
2. *Create* a base wall, as shown in **Figure 6.83**:

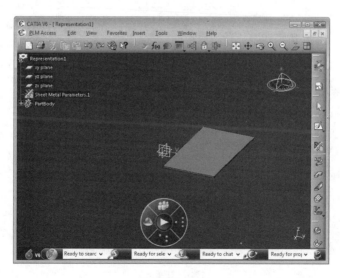

FIGURE 6.83

3. *Select* **Insert**>**Cutting**>**Hole** from the menu bar to create a hole, as shown in **Figure 6.84**:

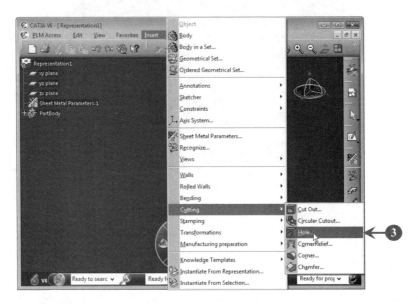

FIGURE 6.84

4. *Select* a point on the base wall where you want to create a hole, as shown in **Figure 6.85**:

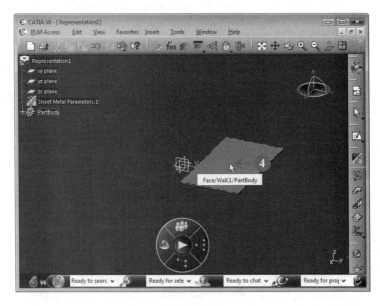

FIGURE 6.85

The **Hole Definition** dialog box opens (**Figure 6.86**).

5. *Enter* a value for the diameter of the hole in the **Diameter** box. In our case, we have entered **20 mm** (Figure 6.86).

6. *Select* the **Type** tab to open the **Type** page, as shown in Figure 6.86:

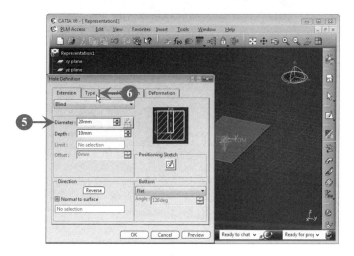

FIGURE 6.86

7. *Select* the type of hole from the drop-down list on the **Type** page. In our case, we have selected **Countersunk**, as shown in **Figure 6.87**:

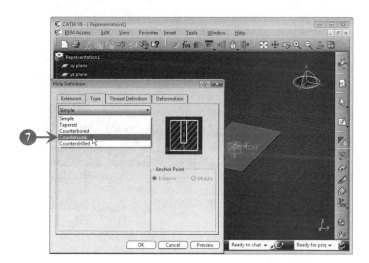

FIGURE 6.87

8. *Click* the **OK** button to close the **Hole Definition** dialog box, as shown in **Figure 6.88**:

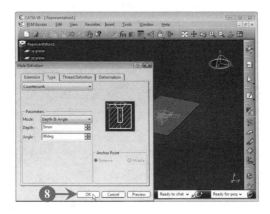

FIGURE 6.88

The countersunk hole is created on the base wall, as shown in **Figure 6.89**:

FIGURE 6.89

We next learn how to create corners on a sheet metal wall.

Creating Corners

Creating corners on a sheet metal wall implies converting a straight-corner sheet metal wall into a rounded-corner sheet metal wall. You can create corners of a specified radius on a sheet metal wall.

Perform the following steps to create corners on a sheet metal wall:

1. *Start* the Generative Sheet Metal Design workbench.
2. *Create* a base wall, as shown in **Figure 6.90**:

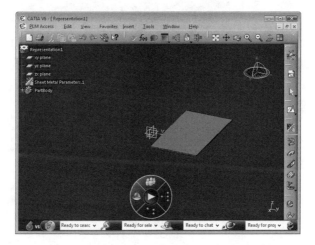

FIGURE 6.90

3. *Select* **Insert > Cutting > Corner** from the menu bar to create corners, as shown in **Figure 6.91**:

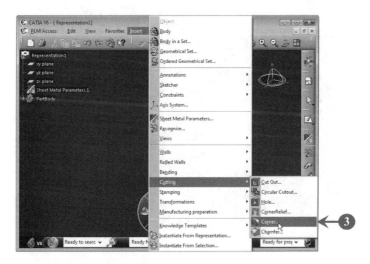

FIGURE 6.91

The **Corner** dialog box opens (**Figure 6.92**).

4. *Enter* a value for the radius of the corners in the **Radius** box. In our case, we have entered **20 mm** (Figure 6.92).

5. *Click* the **Select all** button to select all the corners of the base wall, as shown in Figure 6.92:

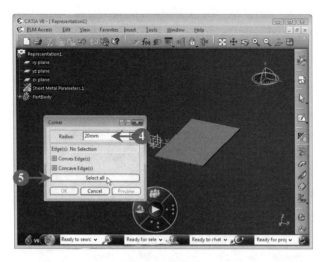

FIGURE 6.92

6. *Click* the **OK** button to close the **Corner** dialog box, as shown in **Figure 6.93**:

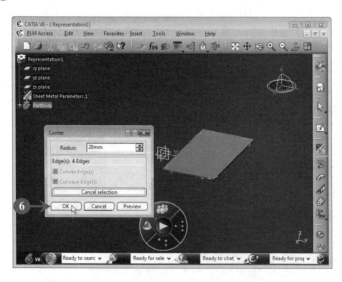

FIGURE 6.93

All four straight corners of the base wall are converted into rounded corners, as shown in **Figure 6.94**:

FIGURE 6.94

We next summarize the main topics covered in this chapter.

SUMMARY

In this chapter, you have learned to create:

- Sheet metal walls
- Bends in sheet metal walls
- Cuts in sheet metal walls

INDEX